First Love
LOST,
True Love
GAINED

How the Creator of the Universe
Led Me Every Step of the Way

REBEKAH WEBB

Olympus Story House
www.olympusstoryhouse.com

Contents

Introduction

*M*y name is Rebekah Webb. My hope is that when you read my story, you will discover what it means to desire God's will above your own. Throughout my life, I have had to surrender my ideas of what I thought my life should be like in order to fully obey and understand what it means to be a servant of Christ.

In this book, I will be discussing one of the most important decisions that anyone has to make: listening to the Father's will when it comes to love. We often have our own ideas of what love should look like and who we should be with. God has a special someone for each of us. The question is, do we decide to do it our way and ultimately mess up? Or do we accept the way of the Lord? For me, I thought I knew exactly who I was going to marry, but it turned out that I was completely wrong.

Even though I was completely wrong, Yahweh corrected my mistakes, just like a wonderful father always does. He led me in every step of the way to meet the man I was intended to marry.

My prayer is that you will trust the Lord for everything in your life, especially when it comes to finding a spouse.

The names of the individuals in this book have been changed to protect their identities.

Chapter 1

A Bit About Me And
How I Met My First Love

*M*y name is Abigail Saba. I grew up in a Christian home with parents who are from two completely different worlds. My mother was born in South Carolina, and my father was born in Syria near the border of Turkey. My father is an Aramean. His name is Andrew Saba. Even though he was born in Syria, he grew up in Lebanon. He has many fascinating stories from living over there. His denomination is Syrian Orthodox. He came to America in 1973 along with many of his relatives, excluding his father who died when he was only fifteen years old. My mother's name is Michelle Saba. Her father was a minister from a Pentecostal background. My mother was the one who always took us to church, so my two sisters and I were basically raised to be Pentecostal.

As a child, I had golden blond hair like the sun and sea-blue eyes. I was a very tough kid, and I hung out with a lot of boys. I enjoyed wrestling, playing basketball, and playing with cars and Batman toys. Yes, I was a tomboy. I thought that the things boys did were more interesting than the things that girls did. I had my first crush on a boy when I was five years old from whom I received a kiss on the cheek. He was such a sweet boy.

I was about seven years old when I gave my life to Christ. For me, God just always seemed to make sense, and I did not need to be convinced. I had seen miracles as a young child, and God began to reveal Himself to me at an early age. During my first time at Bible camp, I received a gift from God. I felt His presence, and as I closed my eyes during prayer time, I saw white all around me. There was such a peace that came over me, and I knew that God was with me. I was baptized when I was eight, along with my ten-year-old sister, Cara. For me, getting baptized was such a blessing. I knew what it meant. It represented on the outside to everyone what had already happened on the inside. God had washed away my sins through the blood of His Son, Jesus.

My sister Cara loved to pick on me. We were complete opposites, from our looks to our ways of doing things, and we fought a lot as children. Our older sister—Laura, who is four years older than me—was very protective. Most of my fights were with Cara, but sometimes Laura would sit on me until I said sorry for whatever I did to offend her. This did not happen very often. Needless to say, I was the type of kid that would not bother you unless you bothered me. However, if you bothered me, I wanted to get revenge. I knew it was horrible to want to get revenge, but I felt like I was itching to get them back, especially Cara. Anyway, this desire to get people back is basically how I met the guy I would one day fall in love with.

I first met Jeffrey Taylor when we were in the sixth grade. He had transferred from a different school and was placed in my social studies class. He was a very scrawny-looking boy with blond hair and blue eyes. He also had this silly little red ring in his ear. I was not sure why, but he decided to pick on me by knocking something off of my table. He thought it was so funny. He then said some ridiculous things to me, and I began to chase him around the room. For some reason or another, the teacher was not in the classroom. This actually happened more than once. Jeffrey just loved to get me frustrated. I, of course, saw the need to get him back. This is basically how our friendship began. I grew accustomed to his constant picking and found out that we actually had some things in common.

Jeffrey and I were friends throughout middle school and into high school. He was not as serious about school until the tenth grade. That is actually when we became more like best friends instead of just friends. We shared a mutual friend who we both hung out with together. His name is Christopher James, but we just call him CJ. I first met CJ in the ninth grade. We got along instantly. He is to this day one of the funniest people I have ever met. CJ had a big crush on me, and he asked me out a few times during high school. I would tell him that I was not interested in dating (especially when he first asked me out in the ninth grade). I am not sure exactly when Jeffrey met CJ, but as a group, we all started hanging out between the ninth and tenth grades.

In the tenth grade, Jeffrey (whom we also called Jeff) had a girlfriend named Hannah. I had heard of her before but had never actually met her, or so I had thought. She lived down the street from Jeff, and they met when she was in the fifth grade, and he was in the sixth. From what I understood from Jeff, they had an "on and off" type of relationship. I actually met her in Spanish class, but I did not yet know that she was his girlfriend. One day during lunch, Jeff introduced us.

He said, "Abigail, this is my girlfriend, Hannah. Hannah, this is my best friend, Abigail."

We both told Jeff that we have Spanish class together. Hannah then made a comment saying, "Now we can talk about Jeffrey behind his back."

I just smiled and shook my head knowing that she was teasing him.

Jeff said, "Oh, great! I should have never introduced you to each other."

We both started laughing. It was fun seeing Jeff get so worked up.

At some point when Jeff, CJ, and I started driving, we would hang out after school. We would usually go over to CJ's house because his house was the halfway point between where I lived and where Jeff lived. We usually would play cards, video games, or watch a movie. Sometimes, Hannah would come to CJ's too. We used to play Black King—a game where if you end up with the Black King at the end of the game, then the winner would get to dare you to do something. Usually, that consisted of bear hugs from CJ (because he was built like a football player), or the dare would be something really cheesy. Anyways, I noticed that when Hannah was at CJ's, she seemed to be jealous of how Jeff would give me more attention than he would her. I basically caught some weird glances from her. I did not pay it much mind as I was not interested in Jeff at the time.

By the time we were in our senior year of high school, we would sometimes still hang out together after school.

Jeff said to me, "Abigail, this is our last year together, and you are my best friend. I want to spend every Saturday with you. It will be our special day together."

I told him, "Jeff, what about Hannah? Shouldn't she come with us? She is your girlfriend after all."

Jeff said, "You are my best friend. You mean more to me than my girlfriend."

Jeff went on to express that he told Hannah that he wanted to spend as much time as he could with me before I went to college next fall. Jeff also said that he told Hannah that if she did not like it, then that's tough. I told Jeff that I would like to talk to Hannah about this first. Jeff told me that her opinion did not matter and that this was between us as best friends. I expressed concern over this and told Jeff that I did not want Hannah to get the wrong idea. Jeff insisted that everything would be fine, and we left it at that.

I went home that day thinking about Jeff's proposal of hanging out without the group. We had all hung out during the summer before our senior year. Jeff and Hannah even came by my house one time so we could ride together to go to a movie. On this particular occasion, my dad was outside, and he came up to Jeff's car as I was about to get in. I noticed that Hannah was in the back seat.

I asked Hannah, "Don't you want to ride up front with Jeff?"

Jeff jumped in before she could speak, and he said, "You are my best friend, so you're riding up front."

I looked at Hannah, and she said, "It's okay. Don't worry about it."

So I just got into the car. Even my dad made a comment about it before we left. When we got to the movie theater, there was still some time before the show, so Jeff had an idea. He saw a photo machine that makes a sketch of the person, and he paid to have my picture taken. While the sketch was being taken, he was messing with my hair in an attempt to make the picture look goofy. I remember looking at Hannah's face, and she seemed upset. I could never understand those two. They seemed to have so many issues in their relationship. So, with this particular outing fresh in my mind, I called Hannah to discuss Jeff's proposal with her.

She told me, "It's fine, Abby. I know that you all are best friends. Besides, you know how Jeff is when he doesn't get his way."

I said, "Yeah, I sure do. He gets really pouty."

We both laughed and ended our conversation on a good note.

Over the next few months, Jeffrey and I had a lot of fun together. We went to the movies, and we played basketball. We even hung out during our study time. We were like two peas in a pod. If we could hang out, we did hang out. As much as I enjoyed spending time with Jeffrey, I could not help but wonder what would become of my friendship with Hannah. I knew in my heart that she was not okay with us hanging out without her. I understood why she was upset, but because I valued my friendship with Jeff above all my other friendships, I did the selfish thing and just put him first. I did not want to waste any time before college. I felt the same as Jeff did in wanting to spend as much time as I could with my best friend. I did not know what would come of all of this, and my heart was not prepared for what would happen next.

Chapter 2

Drama, Drama, and More Drama

*J*ust before winter break, Hannah asked me, "Abigail, do you have feelings for Jeffrey?"

I responded, "No, Hannah, we're just friends."

She said, "Okay."

At that time, I did not have feelings for Jeff, but I knew that I was not making things easier for their relationship. I talked to Jeff that night on the phone about inviting CJ and Hannah to spend time with us on Saturday. Jeff questioned why we would do that when we have so much fun by ourselves. I expressed that while it was true that we have fun together on our own, we were still leaving them out. He said that they could come along sometimes, but that he really just wanted to spend time with me. I explained that I did not want to hurt their feelings by excluding them. We ended the conversation, but I was still troubled by what Hannah said to me. I never imagined my life being full of so much drama, and it was just about to get worse.

A couple of months after winter break, Jeffrey called wanting to go see a movie. I encouraged Jeff to bring Hannah along with us, but he said that they were not getting along at that time. Jeff went on to say that he was upset and wanted to just spend time with me. I really wanted to cheer him up, so I went to the movies with him. During the movie, Jeffrey kept putting his hand out to hold my hand.

I told him, "No, you have a girlfriend. I'm not going to hold your hand."

He kept persisting and giving me this puppy dog look with his beautiful sky-blue eyes as if he were the saddest human being ever. So I gave in and held his hand. I knew I should not have done it as he had a girlfriend who happened to be my friend too. As I was holding his hand, I felt like it was right. We held hands for about twenty minutes or so, and afterward, I didn't feel the same about Jeffrey. I had held hands with guys before; however, I was never serious about any of them. This was my best friend, and after holding his hand that day, I fell in love with him.

I went home and thought about a lot of things. I thought about Hannah and what this would do to her. She had only asked me a couple of months ago whether I had feelings for Jeff. I didn't at that time, but now I do. The next day, I decided to call Ed who was my boyfriend at the time. We only dated for about two months, so it wasn't serious. I told him that we needed to break up because I had feelings for someone else. He seemed okay with it, and that was that. I then called Jeffrey, and without beating around the bush, I told Jeff that after holding his hand I began to have feelings for him. He responded by telling me that he has had a crush on me since the eighth grade. He went on to say that had I not broken my leg during the second half of our eighth-grade year, he would have asked me out. This was shocking to me as I never knew that he liked me in that way. I guess I should have known, but I was blinded at that time.

I expressed to Jeffrey that I didn't want to hurt Hannah and that she had been a good friend to me. Jeff said that the best thing for him to do was to break up with Hannah and not date anyone until he figured out what to do next. I thought that was a good idea, and I expressed how overwhelming all of this was for me. He assured me that everything would be fine. After we got off the phone, I felt so troubled. I felt like such a horrible person for holding his hand. At the same time, I had all these feelings that I had never experienced before. It was all too much, and it was only about to get worse the next day at school.

Jeff and I used to park beside each other in the school parking lot and walk together toward our different classes. Hannah was with him for the ride sometimes, and she was with him that morning. So I figured that everything was okay between them still, but she had an upset look on her face. At that point, I knew that he must have used the car ride to school to break up with her. These two have broken up before, but this time was different, and I was part of the problem. After first period, Hannah and I met up after class.

She asked me, "Abigail, do you know why Jeff broke up with me? He wouldn't give me a reason."

As I looked at her, she was in tears. I had to come clean to her. I told Hannah that the other day when I went to the movies with Jeff, I tried to get her to go with us. I went on to explain that Jeff didn't want her to go due to the fact that they were not getting along and that he insisted on just hanging out with me. I even checked with you, and you said it was fine. She nodded and motioned for me to continue. I then explained while Jeff and I were sitting in the movie theater, Jeff looked really sad and kept giving me this puppy dog look, and he wanted to hold my hand. I told him, "No you have a girlfriend!" Jeff kept insisting, and after a while, I gave in, and I held his hand. I told her that I was so sorry and that I shouldn't have held his hand. Hannah was heartbroken, and she said that I should have told Jeff no, and I should not have held his hand. I again apologized and went on to tell her about the fact that after holding Jeff's hand, I began to have feelings for him.

Hannah was so disappointed; it was only two months ago when she asked me if I had feelings for Jeff. I didn't then, but now I do. What a mess! I told her that I had never meant for this to happen, and I asked for her forgiveness. I went on to tell Hannah that I didn't want to hurt her and that she was my friend. I also explained that Jeff said he doesn't want to date anyone but rather wants to remain friends with both of us.

Hannah said, "You think that makes it better?" She began to cry. Her heart was broken, and I was partly to blame. Hannah suggested that we get to class as we were about fifteen minutes late at that point.

I said, "Okay, I'll see you later."

Hannah, still in tears, said, "Okay, bye."

At lunch, CJ heard the news, and he seemed to be okay with it. He said, "I have always liked you, but if you have to be with another guy, I guess Jeffrey is okay." Jeffrey just smiled, but he wasn't happy because I told Hannah the reason why he broke up with her. Jeff told me that I should have let him tell her in his time. I told him that she deserved to know the truth. The following day, I saw Hannah, and she was very distant and mad at me, which was understandable.

Jeff told me, "Don't worry about her. She's not your best friend, I am."

I was still so heartbroken for her, and I hated that I upset her so much. In Chemistry class, I began to cry, and my teacher, Ms. Porter, said, "What's wrong, Abigail? Why are you so upset?"

I gave her a brief summary of what happened, and I told her, "I feel like such a horrible person, and I never meant for this to happen."

Ms. Porter gave me a hug and assured me that everything would be okay in due time. I stopped crying as class was about to begin, but I could not see a better day heading my way. There was just too much drama, and I felt like I was the center of it all.

Hannah and I had the same Spanish class, so we had to see each other there. It was like being on a deserted island. She looked at me, and I felt the cold in her eyes. I never knew what it felt like to be hated in someone's eyes until that day. I had betrayed our friendship, and she was not going to let it go, at least for now anyway. I did the only thing I could do, which was the only thing that made sense to me at that moment. I opened up my Bible and began to read it. I read all of Song of Solomon in class that day. The teacher kept telling me to put it away and that I needed to do my work, but I couldn't focus on anything else. I needed to be comforted, and Spanish class wasn't going to give me comfort, not with Hannah looking at me with those cold eyes. Instead, I read the Bible and ignored my teacher.

After Spanish class, it was lunchtime, and Jeff and CJ were at our usual table. I got a sub and sat down. They waited for me to pray so we could all eat together as was our custom. I sat down and said, "Dear Heavenly Father, thank You for the food, and please bless it to the nourishment of our bodies and to your service in Jesus's name, amen." We all ate, and CJ suggested that we all get away from the drama and go see a movie that night. Jeff and I agreed. When we got to the theater, Jeff sat between CJ and me. The movie happened to be a romantic comedy, and there were moments where I began to cry because of all the things going on between me, Hannah, and Jeff. Jeff put his arm around me, and he tried to comfort me.

He said, "You mean so much to me. I don't want to lose my best friend."

I reciprocated the same feelings back to him. He then hugged me, and we held hands again. After the movie, we hugged and thanked CJ for the idea that night. It had made things better between Jeff and me. It was good to get away from the drama, but I could not escape it for long. After all, there is always tomorrow.

Chapter 3

My Heart Says, "I Do!"

Over the next few weeks, there were no repairs to my friendship with Hannah. She continued to give me evil looks, and at one point, she even cursed at me as I walked down the hallway. Jeff insisted that I just ignore Hannah. I decided to take his advice and try to move past all of this. After I moved on from all that drama, things began to look up for me. I decided to focus on my schoolwork and, of course, my relationship with Jeff. I began to picture my future with Jeff, and I even wrote my name as "Abigail Taylor" in my notebook. I wanted to marry my best friend one day. I kept this to myself, at least from my parents anyway.

I saw myself getting more and more attached to Jeff. I wanted to hang out with him even more than before. One night, I fell asleep while watching a movie at his house, and I missed curfew. My dad was upset at me and rightfully so. I expressed how sorry I was and that I had fallen asleep while watching a movie. My parents trusted me as I had never done anything to betray their trust. Jeff called me one night wanting to hang out, but it was a school night. He suggested that I ask my parents if I could come over to study. I told him that I would ask them, but I doubted that they would allow it since it was already eight o'clock.

So I said to my dad, "Hey, Baba (which is Lebanese for *dad*), can I go to my friend's house and study?"

He said, "No! What's the matter with you? Don't you know what time it is?"

I said, "Okay, I was just asking, sorry."

I told Jeff that we would have to wait until tomorrow to hang out at school. Jeff understood, but he was disappointed that I could not come over.

As I drew closer to Jeff, my relationship with God began to be affected. I still read my Bible and prayed, but I didn't feel like I was putting God first. Jeff was definitely the center of my attention. I felt like he was the one for me, and I didn't care about his flaws. For one, he smoked cigarettes, which for me is a huge problem because I am allergic to cigarette smoke. Ever since I was a baby, I would get ear infections from others smoking around me. My father quit smoking when I was a year old, and many of my ear infections subsided. Even today, when anyone smokes around me, I feel a burning sensation in my throat and ears, my nose starts to get stuffed, and it becomes difficult to breathe. Jeff knew of my allergy to cigarettes, and he would always sit away from me when he did smoke.

There were a couple of times where Jeff leaned over while we were watching a movie at his house, and he tried to kiss me. I would not let him. The idea of kissing him was gross. I had never kissed a guy before (I wanted my first kiss to be with the man who I was going to marry), and he smoked cigarettes. Even though my heart was crazy about Jeff, my head was still like, *I don't know*. My head was what kept me together. The other problem was that we were headed down different paths. I was going to ministry school in the fall, and he was going to work full time at his grandparents' cleaning business. All I knew at the time was that I enjoyed his company, and my heart was what kept me wanting to spend more and more time with him.

I had Algebra II with CJ where we had made a mutual friend named Jessica Young. Jessica is a Christian who is very funny and sweet. She invited CJ and me to go to her church for a youth function, and we had a blast. There were water balloon fights, races, and, of course, food. Our friendship grew with Jessica, and she quickly became one of our best friends. Soon we would introduce her to Jeffrey. During Algebra II class, CJ asked me if I would go to prom with him. At that time, Jeff and I had already decided not to go to prom. We just wanted to hang out with each other as we both didn't care for dancing and getting dressed up. I told CJ that I appreciated the offer, but that it wasn't my scene. I then suggested that he should ask Jessica to the prom. I believed they would have a great time together. CJ took my advice and asked Jessica, and she was incredibly happy to go to the prom with him.

On prom night, Jeff and I hung out, and we listened to music in my Jeep. We put the seats down and looked at the stars. Jeff started to sing this song with a high-pitched voice, trying to imitate the female vocalist, and we both started laughing. Jeff was always good at making me laugh. We could talk about anything. However, Jeff also began to complain there was nothing to do, and my suggestions to go to the movies or to get something to eat did not seem to extinguish those laments. Later that night, Jeff had to go and help Hannah. She was locked out of her house, and Hannah needed a place to stay until her mother got home from work. So our day ended in a very awkward way with us arguing over his incessant complaining. I thought it was just lame, and I began to think that I should have just gone to prom with CJ. After all, it would have been better than dealing with this. CJ and Jessica had a great time at the prom, and they showed me their pictures. I was happy for them. Soon afterward, Jeff and I patched things up. It was hard to stay mad at him.

By graduation time, Jeff had already met Jessica. CJ and I invited Jessica to go to our graduation (she was in the eleventh grade). We all took pictures together along with some of our other friends. It was a joyous occasion. We would all be moving on and heading to different places in our lives. CJ would be attending college in the fall. He wanted to be a history major. I would be going to a ministry school that was both full-time Bible college and full-time ministry. It was basically Bible boot camp. I had decided on this college by praying and "The Mission" was the school for me. In no time at all, Jeff moved to the next city over, and he rented a trailer there. It belonged to his mother, and she rented it to him. I went there a couple of times during the summer. He kept the place in tip-top condition. He was particularly good at cleaning.

I went to Jeff's family gathering one time. On the way there, he gave me a disk that he made just for me. It had all of my favorite Christian bands on it. His little brother was in the back seat.

His little brother said, "Aww, that's so sweet."

Jeff said, "Shut up, Carl, and mind your business."

I thought it was sweet, and we held hands on the way to his relatives' house. When we got there, they were all staring at me. I wasn't Hannah, and they were used to seeing her with Jeff. Jeff introduced me to everyone and said, "Hey, everyone, this is my best friend, Abigail."

I just said, "Hi everyone."

I had already met his mother Valerie and her friend Rachel. They both loved me and thought I was good for Jeff.

They told Jeff, "She's got a good head on her shoulders. She's a keeper." He smiled with pride when they said that.

One summer day, Jeff and I were hanging out, and I wanted to go to a car show. He did not want to go, and he came up with this lame excuse of not being able to buy a car that he might like. I told him that I just like looking at old cars and that I really wanted to go. He declined and would not go. I was upset at him, and I said, "Okay, well I want to go home."

So he exclaimed, "Fine, I'll take you home then!"

Usually, when we had a fight, we got over it pretty quickly. However, this time was different as we were both using the silent treatment.

As Jeff and I were no longer on speaking terms, I grew closer to CJ. While CJ and I were at the movie theater one night, he asked me if I would be his girlfriend. I had said no to him at other times, but this time I thought to myself, *I should give him a chance as he has always been a good friend to me.* So I told him, "Yes, but on one condition. I want it to be based on our friendship."

He agreed and was so happy. CJ and I had a great time together over the summer. We went to play pool, and he often won. He was an incredibly talented pool player, and I learned a lot from him.

One day, Bobby, who is like a younger brother to me, came over to my house to spend the night. Bobby was fourteen years old at the time and about six inches taller than me. That night, I told CJ that we should meet up to play pool, and I brought Bobby with me. Bobby kept getting on CJ's nerves the whole night. After we played pool, we went to see a movie. Bobby saw CJ holding my hand at the movie theater, and then he decided to hold my hand as a joke. I thought it was funny. I have known Bobby since he was like four or five years old. Then Bobby put his arm around me, and CJ was like, "Okay, that's it." He moved his arm away, and I just laughed. Bobby was a teaser, and he wanted to get CJ worked up. CJ has a little brother, and he wasn't going to put up with Bobby's nonsense. It was a fun night, and that was the last time we had a date like that.

It was almost the end of the summer right before college was about to start, and Jeff called me up and said, "I miss you, and I don't want you to go to college without saying goodbye to me."

I told him, "I have missed you too."

So we met up at the park, and we hugged and talked about all the fun we had during our senior year. He had just gotten a cell phone, so he gave me his number so that we could keep in touch. It was both a happy and sad day at the same time. I was happy to be in a good relationship with Jeff, and I still loved him even though I had been going out with CJ. I was sad because it would be a while before I could see him again.

Later on that night, I met up with CJ. He had given me his class ring, and I wanted to give it back. I explained to him that I couldn't keep something that valuable and that we had to break up. He asked why, and I explained to him that the ministry program that I was going to did not allow their students to date. This was true for both first-year and second-year students.

He said, "Well, I can wait for you."

I told CJ that it would not be fair to him and that we should just be friends. He wasn't happy about it, but he seemed to understand. There was a fork in the road, and we were both heading to different colleges. Not to mention, my heart still said, "I do!" when it came to Jeffrey Taylor.

Chapter 4

The Fight In My Heart
For First Place

When I first arrived at the Mission school, it was August of 2004. My mother was with me that day to help me get settled into my dorm room. She also stayed for orientation. It was great to have her there with me. As they began to read off the rules, there were several rules that I needed help with. The main one was modesty. That day, I was wearing a low-cut V-neck shirt that showed my cleavage. It was so low that they took my ID picture from the neck up. At that time, I didn't think it was a problem to dress that way. The rule was that girls needed to wear undershirts, and it was done to protect the eyes of our brothers in Messiah. I, of course, complied, but I knew that it was going to take some getting used to. The other rule was the no-dating policy. I was fine with this rule because the guy who I was in love with was not at this program.

After orientation, we were introduced to our group leaders. I was in a group with five others, and our leader's name was Jim. Jim asked us if we needed to be broken of anything. I really didn't know how or even why I should respond to that question after just meeting the group and Jim. When it was my turn to speak, I simply just said no. At that time, I was not willing to let anyone pry into my life. It was just too soon.

After a couple of months into the Mission program, I needed to have a heart-to-heart with God. I felt so distant from Him even though I was serving God in a full-time capacity. It was like He was giving me the cold shoulder treatment. One day, I had some private time in my dorm room, and I began to seek God's face. I prayed, and I didn't stop seeking God and His forgiveness. Then He finally spoke to my heart. I was again in the right relationship with Him. It was revealed to me that I needed to get away from Jeff so that God could be first in my life again. I told Yahweh that I was sorry for hurting Him by putting Jeff before Him. After I repented, things began to change in my heart. I really started to grow in my relationship with God, and it was amazing to see how He was using me to help others.

I had made some really good friends at the Mission school. They were so different from my friends back home. I had more in common with my college friends because we all had the same purpose in mind. We were there to serve God and to help others, and that's exactly what we did. This school was both full-time ministry and full-time schooling. We didn't have much time to do what we wanted. It was about helping the poor, the lost, and the brokenhearted. In my first year, I was assigned to a team where we went to help out in the inner-city projects with children. It was so sad to see all these children living around drugs and violence. Some children as young as four years old would cuss you out as if that were a normal thing to do. It was how they were brought up. Over time, as we worked with the children, some began to change. We showed them love, and they no longer saw the need to hold hatred in their little hearts.

My parents bought me a cell phone after being in the Mission for a couple of months. It was a complete surprise. Before that, I was only able to talk to them when the landline was available in the main foyer. Having a cell phone made it easier for me to talk to Jeff. I loved talking to Jeff. We would talk for as long as we could. It always seemed like the whole world would disappear, and it was just us. We had so much fun goofing off and talking about anything and everything. I missed him so much, and I couldn't wait to see him during winter break.

Over winter break, Jeff, CJ, Jessica, and I met up and exchanged gifts. It was a joyous occasion, and we had many laughs. Jeff noticed that I was different in the way that I dressed and in the way I responded to certain jokes.

He said, "You've changed. You don't dress the same, and you don't act the same."

I responded, "I am just more in love with God and the things of God than what I was before."

At first, my statement seemed to bother him, but he got over it once we hung out at the movies on our own. He always liked taking me to the movies. We didn't watch movies like normal people. We would make jokes, and we would share nachos and a drink. He always wanted me to take two nachos and make them look like a duck. Goofing off was our specialty, and we served it up every time we were together. It was so hard to go back to the Mission after seeing Jeff, but my desire to serve God and to do His will was stronger than the feelings I had for Jeff.

We received some strange news after coming back from winter break. Our school would be relocating to another city about an hour away. What was even more strange was that we would all be living in different host homes for the next couple of months until the place we would be living in was up to code. I was assigned to live in a studio apartment–like place with five other girls out in the country. It was nice to be in the country, but there was literally no privacy. I would often go outside to talk on the phone to Jeff. I would also go out every night, make some hot tea, and wrap myself up in a blanket while reading the Bible and talking to God. One of the girls would tease me and say, "Abigail is going outside to talk to the cows again." I would just smile at her as she liked to kid about everything.

One night, I called Jeff and talked to him for an hour or so. We talked about a lot of things including our future. Jeff told me that he didn't think he was good enough for me. I told him that he was good enough for me and that I loved him. I also encouraged him with sweet words, and then he felt better about himself. I simply refused to give up on the idea of us being together one day. After the main house was up to code and we all moved in, it made things even more difficult to talk to Jeff. Imagine being in a house with thirty-plus people. The guys stayed downstairs and the girls upstairs. It was a really big house, but I was kind of missing the other place already.

One night, during a church event known as Kids Quest, I met a girl named Daisy. She was only six years old. She sat beside me and began jumping up and down on the church pews. I told her to sit down, and then she sat on the floor. I told her that it was fine for her to sit on the floor. She then pouted for a little bit. Then the speaker called the workers to come to the front to lead the children in prayer. To my surprise, Daisy came to me for prayer time. Only she did not seem to really want to pray. Instead, she told me, "If you want, you can come to my house, and I will cook you some eggs." I was stunned as I have never had a kid tell me that. From that day forward, Daisy became like a little sister to me.

On May 5, 2005, I wrote in my journal these exact words,

> Today at prayer time I prayed for many people, but I really began to pray for two lost souls in particular. One being my sister Cara and the other being my best friend, Jeffrey. I know that both of them are going to be saved. It's kind of hard for me to pray for Jeff's salvation sometimes because it seems like I want him to be saved for two reasons. One so that he can have a relationship with God, and two so that I might actually be united with him in marriage someday. I realized today I was wrong in this pursuit. There was a time in my life where I had put Jeff before God. I loved Jeff with all my heart, and I never felt something quite like it. I also felt God's presence during that time when I fell for Jeff and even after I fell for him. Jeff and Hannah have not been together for a little over a year now. I tried to talk to Hannah, but she is still very bitter towards me. I know that God will heal her heart.

Today, I asked God to take away any thoughts of me being with Jeff if he is not the one for me. God told me tonight, that I was not ready to know who was for me, and that He was not going to let me know until I was ready. I trust God in this and everything else in my life. Proverbs 3:5–6

As summer break was approaching, I couldn't wait to get home to see my family and friends. They had a ceremony for all the first and second-year students. Jeff and my family came. It was so good to see Jeff and that he was supporting me. When I got home and started going to work with my dad, I began to feel very distraught all of a sudden. I have worked with my dad for years, and I knew he needed my help. However, something was pulling me in a different direction. I felt like I was in a place of confusion. I couldn't concentrate on anything, so I began to read the Bible almost nonstop. I just wanted some relief, some kind of an answer. I felt like I was going crazy.

After dealing with this for about three days, I decided to ask God why I was feeling this way? He showed me (as I had my eyes closed) a picture of Daisy, and that I needed to return to the Mission and be a part of the summer team. My friend Mary from the Mission was also going to be there during the summer. When I told my dad, he was upset with me. However, I reminded him of a promise that I made to God when I was fourteen years old. I said, "I will go wherever You want me to go. I will say whatever You want me to say. Just send me, and I will do it."

My dad already knew about the vow I made to God, but he didn't understand why I had to go then. My mom has always been more supportive of my vow to the Lord, and she understood why I needed to return to the Mission for the summer.

Chapter 5

Fully Devoted To God's Will

This was the first summer where I would not be spending as much time with my family and friends. My time would be spent serving God and learning to be completely devoted to doing His will. I still had Jeff on my mind, but he was not the front runner anymore. God was now in first place, and I wanted Him to stay in first place.

Over the summer, I had some fights with my friend Mary. She kept sticking her nose in places it did not belong. Mary kept making comments about Jeff, particularly why I should not be interested in him due to the fact that he is not a Christian. I told her I had been praying for him to get saved, and that I was not interested in any other guy at that time. It was not like Jeff was constantly on my mind anymore, but he was definitely a part of my heart's desire. My main focus was to minister to Daisy as that was after all why God had called me here for the summer.

Our ministry team held an event at the apartment complex where Daisy lived. When Daisy saw me, she gave me a big hug. She stayed by my side during the Bible lesson. During the lesson, the children were all sitting in a circle, and the teacher asked for them to take as many squares from the toilet paper roll as they wanted. When it was Daisy's turn, I told her, "Just take one piece." So she did.

Then the teacher explained, "With the number of squares of toilet paper you have, tell me what you know about God."

Now Daisy's mom was in the room, and she was a Muslim. Daisy asked me, "What should I say?"

I told her to say that Jesus is the Son of God. So she did, and her mother said, "No, He isn't! Jesus is a prophet."

Then Daisy said, "No, Mom! Jesus is the Son of God!"

Her mother was silenced. I was so amazed at the boldness of this child. She was not afraid to tell her mother that she was wrong and that she believed in Jesus. I knew that the main reason God had called me back for the summer was to minister to his precious child, Daisy.

Besides ministering to Daisy, I helped out at various church camps where I did drama ministry with the summer team. It was a blast to get to travel and spend time with my friends while doing ministry at various churches. We also had an end-of-the-summer event for the inner-city community where Daisy and I spent the day together. It was great getting to see her smile and laugh all day long.

Summer went by so fast, and now it was time to get back to school and ministry at the same time. My second year of the Mission was nothing like my first year. I was made a group leader along with three other second-year students. We had to lead a team of five to six people. My group was called "Koinonia," meaning fellowship in Greek. We got along well with each other. Our job as a group was to cook and clean on alternating weeks with the other teams. We also played team sports together, and we had meetings together to improve our communications. My friend Will (who was also a second-year student) and I were in charge of both the drama team and recruitment. We stayed extremely busy. Sometimes we would be up past midnight working on dramas. We traveled to several churches, and we had to keep on top of our schoolwork at the same time. It was definitely a challenge, but I was focused on doing God's will, and I had a strong desire to help others.

After we did dramas, there was always a sermon given by Brother Jim. During altar calls, God would usually give me discernment as to whom I should speak and pray with. There was a girl at one of the churches who seemed so cold at the altar, and she was just standing around. I went up to her, and I asked if she needed prayer for anything, and she said, "No, I'm okay."

I stood and talked with her for a moment, and I expressed that I felt like there was something not right. I asked her if everything was okay, and then the girl began to cry. She told me that her dad had just died a month ago and that she was angry with God for taking him away. I stated how sorry I was for her loss. Then I asked the girl if her dad had a relationship with God, and she nodded her head yes. I encouraged her to give all her anger to God and to cry it out to Him. She did, and after that, she felt better. This was just one example of the many teenage girls that I would go on to help throughout that year at the Mission. I helped girls who struggled with bulimia, girls who wanted to run away from home, and those who wanted to hurt themselves. It was a blessing to get to be used by God, not only on stage but also off stage. Off the stage, I could really impact a person's life just by taking the time to listen to their problems.

It was ironic to me how I could connect with and help so many girls while the issues which existed between me and my friend Mary seemed to linger. Mary was the leader of all the girls including me, and she could be very snooty at times. One night, when I was on the phone with Jeff, she got onto me about it. Lights out was at 10:00 p.m., unless there was prep work for drama ministry. I was up past that time, speaking with Jeff, and Mary told me that I needed to end my phone call. I told her that I was being quiet, and it was the weekend, which was the only time to catch up with friends. Jeff suggested that I go and hit Mary with a pillow. At first, I did not want to do that, but eventually, I did hit her with a pillow. Mary could be downright rude sometimes, and it felt good to let out some stress with a simple smack of a pillow. Jeff thought it was funny while Mary became irritated, but she got over it. Jeff always had a way of getting me to do silly things like that.

In January 2006, my sister Cara had her second child. To my surprise, Mary wanted to go with me to visit my sister and to meet my new niece, Rachel, at the hospital. Even though Mary and I had our issues, we were still there for one another when it mattered. When we arrived at the hospital, my sister was really exhausted.

She had to have a cesarean due to some complications during the birthing process. Rachel was such a beautiful blond-haired and blue-eyed baby girl. I was so thrilled for my sister. Children are such a gift from God. Mary was very passionate about standing up for children's rights, and she made it a priority to attend the walk for life rally in Washington, D.C. that year. She also organized a day where students held pro-life signs along the side of one of the busy streets in Lynchburg, Virginia. I got to be a part of it. Mary was an inspiration, and her passion for helping others was contagious.

I went to a conference in Georgia with some of the students and ministry leaders from my school. While there, I met a group of ministers who were associated with YUGO ministries. YUGO Ministries is an organization that focuses on ministering to people in Mexico. I received some information about their summer staffing program, and I began to pray if it was right for me. All second-year students were required to go on a missions trip. Usually, the Mission group would go to Abaco, Bahamas. I did not feel like I was supposed to go there. As I prayed about Mexico, the desire became stronger and stronger. At first, my friend Will was interested in going, but he eventually decided that it was not right for him at that time.

When I finally decided that I was going, I applied, and they accepted me into the staffing program. When I told Pastor Robert, the director of the Mission, about YUGO ministries, he was disappointed. Pastor Robert explained that I should have let him check it out first. Then he told me that he would look into it just to make sure it was a good option for my mission's trip. I felt confident that it would be just the right place for me to go. After checking it out, he said it was a reputable organization and that I would be fine going there. I was thankful for his input as I knew he had my best interest at heart. Now, I just had to get my parents on board and, of course, raise the money necessary for the trip.

When I told my parents, my mom was fine with it, and she encouraged me to go. My father, on the other hand, was quite upset about it. He said, "Tijuana is a dangerous place!" In the end, he was supportive of my decision as he usually is. Right after finding out about going to Mexico, the director of the Mission school told us that our school would be relocating once again. However, this time, the school would be in Baltimore, Maryland. I could not believe it. I had already decided that I was going to stay on as a third year, and I would be going to Liberty University off campus. Now I had to do some praying once more about whether I would stay in Lynchburg, Virginia, or go and be a third year at the Mission in Baltimore.

As I prayed over the matter for a few days, I came to realize that God wanted me to go to Baltimore. My mother told me that she knew I was not going to go to Liberty University. My dad, who was already upset about Mexico, was even more disappointed about me going to Baltimore. He said, "Do you know how dangerous Baltimore is? What are you trying to do to me?"

My mother told him that God would protect me. After my dad calmed down, he told me that he was going to give me the Jeep to take to Baltimore after getting back from Mexico. I was so grateful. I knew it was hard for him to support my decision even though it was all about serving God.

There was just one problem, I was going to miss Daisy and all the other kids who I taught on Wednesday nights. I spent as much time with Daisy as I could before having to head home and get ready for Mexico. God showed me that Daisy would be in good hands. He had put other people in her life who were doing His will and that I did not need to worry about her. It was still hard to think that I would never see her again, but she will always be a part of my prayer life.

After graduation, I only had a few days at home with my family. I was going to miss them so much. It would be another summer away from home, but much further from home this time. My parents took me to the airport and kissed and hugged me goodbye. This was going to be the first time I have been so far away from anyone I knew.

I landed in San Diego on June 11, 2006. This would be the first time that I would be doing ministry so far from home. I didn't feel scared or alone because I knew that God had plans for me that summer. While in Mexico, I met some really amazing people. People who would challenge me and even sharpen me. My roommate Beth was very outspoken and didn't hesitate to question my doctrine. She was Baptist, and I was, of course, Pentecostal, so we tended to butt heads on various subjects in the Scripture. We had some great times still, and we laughed about plenty. I was a part of three different teams at YUGO ministries. One was kitchen duty, another was latrine, and the third was women's ministry.

Each week, we would have different youth groups come to the YUGO ranch, and they would stay in tents. Our job was to prepare them and take care of their needs so that they could minister to the Mexican people. These kids would have to help with kitchen duty and bathroom duty. I was responsible for teaching and encouraging the girls during bathroom duty. There were a few girls who wrote notes, thanking me for encouraging them. They were so sweet. I really enjoyed helping out with the women's ministry. We would do a Bible study and teach them how to sew. There was a craft in which we taught the women how to make a felt calendar. Each day of the week, girls would come in to learn something new, and then they would go and teach it to the Mexican ladies in the neighborhoods. There were also different ministers that would come to the camp, bringing encouragement and teaching the importance of the Great Commission.

There were two weeks where youth groups didn't come in, and we held a vacation Bible school in this neighborhood. I had never seen homes like I saw in that neighborhood. The houses looked as though they shouldn't be standing, but somehow it all worked out. At VBS, this girl named Abigail formed a bond with me, and she gave me a jewelry set. It was so precious. I thought to myself, *This child does not have much, but she still has it in her heart to bless me.* I also was able to teach a lesson in Spanish. It was interesting and somewhat uncomfortable, but I managed to get through it. We also visited an orphanage several times, and it was amazing to see how well behaved these children were. They were so sweet and so very well taken care of. The orphanage was a part of YUGO ministries. They had planned to set up an adult's home near the orphanage where the elderly could be blessed by the children and vice versa.

I could write about so much more of all the ministry and lessons that I had learned while in Mexico but that would be an exceptionally long story. However, I will say that I was greatly challenged. While there, I read about ten chapters in the Bible every day. It was a great time to be alone with my Heavenly Father and to draw closer to His will for my life. This was a summer I would never forget, and I could not wait for whatever new adventures I would be having when I arrived in Baltimore. On my last night in Mexico, my friends stayed up so that they could send me off with some hugs. I was going to miss them so much. I felt so blessed to have this amazing experience with such wonderful people. Thankfully, we would keep in touch by phone or email.

After saying my goodbyes, I headed to the airport to go home. When I arrived at the airport on August 10, 2006, to meet my parents, my little niece Emily was with them. It was the best surprise ever. I missed all of them so much. After visiting with my family and having an amazing home-cooked meal, I got together with my friends Jeff and Jessica. I kept in touch somewhat with them when we would go to San Diego each week to make a shopping run. Finally, I would be getting to actually spend time with them face-to-face. I gave them some gifts from Mexico, and I told them some stories. I also gave a metal-shelled Bible to Jeff. He thought it was a great gift. I felt like he was supposed to have it. We joked around and had some great fun. I would have loved to spend more time with them, but I only had a few days before going to Baltimore on the fifteenth. I was going to miss my friends, and it would be a while before I could see them again.

My heart was still beating toward Jeff. I just couldn't let him go. In my mind, he was the one for me, and I never imagined loving anyone like I loved him. Putting my feelings for Jeff aside, I had to focus on getting ready for Baltimore. While I was excited, I was also nervous as my dad had made it sound so scary. I would also have to find employment and figure out which online school I should enroll in. I didn't have much time for any kind of prep work in Mexico, so I was feeling really rushed at this point. Even though I felt rushed, I knew I would be okay once I got settled in. My time was not my own anymore. I was driven by God, and I was on His time clock. Baltimore, here I come.

Chapter 6

My Heart Says, "Yes!" But What Does God Say?

*I*t was time to go to Baltimore, and my parents went with me. My dad wanted to make sure I got there safely, and I was glad because I had never driven that far before. When I arrived there, I was so excited to see my friends. It had been a long two months, and I was eager to tell them about the ministry trip to Mexico. After getting settled in, my parents and I said our goodbyes with hugs and kisses, then they headed back home. I was going to miss them so much. I didn't get to spend much time with them over the summer, and now my school was much further away. This was going to be a vastly different and exciting year in which I would have much more responsibility as an intern.

All the students, interns, and leaders gathered together in the meeting area, which was like a sanctuary. We literally were living in a church. Our leader, Robert Benson, began telling us what ministries we would be plugged into this year, and what churches we would be helping out at. I was given two roles, one being Celebrate Recovery and the other being children's ministry. I was really excited about helping out at Celebrate Recovery as it would be a whole new experience, and I loved helping people. However, I felt like I should be doing something other than working with children. So I talked to the director, and he said I could help out at the soup kitchen instead.

To me, that was perfect as I loved being able to help the poor. It was such a blessing to get to do ministries that were so close to my heart.

Now it was time to look for a job. My friend Paul and I went to apply at Target together. After a week went by, I went to Target to inquire about the job. They interviewed me on the spot, and I was hired. I would not start working until early September, which was less than a week away. I told my friend Paul that I was hired, and he went to Target and was hired too. It was such a blessing to have work. I was so thankful to God for answering my prayer in finding a job. I would later come to find out that this was not just going to be a job, but another way to minister to people.

It was August 28, 2006, and I had some things on my mind. I began to ask God about marriage again. I said, "God, if Jeffrey Taylor and I are never to be together, please reveal it to me today or when You think I am ready to hear."

Yahweh did not tell me that day whether I would be united with Jeff in marriage or not. I guess I was not ready to hear it yet. However, my heart was being prepared to hear what the Heavenly Father's will was for me in this matter.

On September 3, 2006, while I was in church that morning, God spoke to me and said, "You will never be with Jeffrey Taylor. You will never marry him."

This news was devastating at the time, but I knew that I had to do God's will. No matter how much it hurt, and no matter how much I loved Jeffrey, I had to say yes to the Heavenly Father. That night, and for the next several nights, I cried myself to sleep, listening to a song by Shekinah Glory called "Yes." The lyrics that touched my heart and really helped me the most from the song were, "Just say yes, open up your heart and tell the Lord yes." I had never felt like this before, and I still loved Jeffrey so much. Being told "No!" was the hardest thing I have ever had to hear from God. I did not know how I was going to tell Jeff. My heart was broken, and I needed to accept it before telling him. The worst part of all this was that I kept this to myself. I just needed time to process it all. I kept thinking about the question I asked God just a few days ago about Jeffrey. I didn't feel ready, but God knew I could handle it.

After about a week of crying over Jeffrey, I finally got the courage and strength to call him. I told him, "God spoke to me and said that we cannot be together, and I can never marry you."

Jeffrey said, "Maybe God is just testing us to see if we will keep strong."

I told him, "I hope that is what it is, but for some reason, I feel that God has other people for us to be with."

He then stated, "God does work in mysterious ways. Do you think God will change His mind?"

I replied to him, "I hope so. We will just have to continue to pray about the situation."

Jeff went on to tell me that we would always be best friends no matter what and that he loved me. This comforted me, and I responded to him in like manner. It made me so happy to hear him say we would remain as best friends. I loved Jeffrey so much, and I would have been the happiest girl if God had let me be his wife. For some reason, God had some other people planned for us. I felt more comfortable with Jeffrey than any other person I had met in my life. I guessed that God would one day let me see comfort in the arms of another man.

That was by far one of the most difficult conversations I have ever had with Jeffrey. I felt so hurt inside, and after expressing that hurt to my best friend, it broke his heart. This was devastating to us both. However, God knew that we were not meant for each other. The Lord had someone else in mind for me, and I had to submit to His will and say, "Yes," no matter how much it hurt at that time.

As the weeks passed by, Jeff and I still spoke on the phone, but it was not the same. I did not have him in my heart like before. Nevertheless, he was still in my mind, and the love I had for him had not left yet. I guess if you have loved someone for such a long time, they stay with you in a way. I did not know how I was ever going to find someone else that could mean as much to me as Jeff did. Jeff knew everything about me. He knew what made me happy and what made me sad. He knew how to make me laugh, and we did a lot of laughing. I would come to find out really soon that what I really wanted in a husband did not look anything like Jeff. God began to prepare my heart and to show me what qualities I needed to find in a husband. Questions began to fill my mind. What would my husband be like? Would we do ministry together? Is he someone who I already know? I had so many questions, and all I needed to really do was to stop being anxious and to wait and trust in God to reveal everything in His timing.

Chapter 7

---

5 Qualities That I Want In A Husband

Over the next few weeks, I became so busy working at Target and doing full-time ministry that I did not have much time to think about Jeffrey. I still called him, but it was just me talking to my buddy, and that was it.

Anyways, God began to show me that I needed to write down five qualities that I wanted in a husband. I never thought about writing down what I wanted in a husband before, so this idea was completely new to me. I began to pray about what I wanted in a husband, and this is what I wrote.

Five qualities that I want in a husband are as followes:

1. For him to follow after God wholeheartedly. A man after God's own heart.
2. For him to have the Word in his heart. Not just reading it but receiving it. Through his dedication in reading the Bible, he practices and lives out God's Word.
3. For him to want to share in a partnership with me in Christ. Serving Christ for the rest of our lives.

4. For him to be responsible in a way that is pleasing to God. A man who pays back what is due and who saves according to God's plan for his life and the lives of others (Luke 12:48).
5. For us to share in the blessing of our friendship. That is a friendship that we share through Christ. His personality must be stubborn in a good way (a strengthening way). A funny man who has such joy and love in his heart for me and others. I want him to be my best friend, and he must be cute to me.

After I had written down these qualities, I began to think about the man who would one day become my husband. It was like a light switch went off toward Jeffrey, and another one was turned on by God to lead me to my future husband. It was so exciting, but I kept all these things in my heart as I waited for the day that I would meet my spouse.

On October 29, 2006, God revealed something to me, and so I wrote it down.

Just as I (God), am preparing my bride (church), I am sending people to tend to her needs so that as she grows, she will be radiant. I send her presents, wrapped in the first wrapping paper that when the present is opened everyone who sees gets to take a piece of the wrapping paper which exposes the gift. I am sending her (church) mentors, leaders of all kinds to build and encourage her, so that she will become stronger in Me. She will look at Me with all her passion. "If any man should come after Me, he must deny himself take up his cross daily and follow Me" (Luke 9:23). In the same way, Abigail, I am sending you a husband. I am preparing his heart and your heart right now. So as you draw closer to

Me and he draws closer to Me, then your love for one another will be expressed, and the dedication of marriage will be established.

I then wrote in gratitude toward God,

Thank you, Jesus, for helping me to see today. I really needed that. Amen!

When God spoke to me that day, He brought so much encouragement to me. I felt even more excited about marriage, and I knew that God was walking me through every step of the way. When He says, "I will never leave you nor forsake you," He really means it.

I began to miss going to Spanish church, so I found one and decided to attend. A friend of mine from the Mission wanted to go with me. His name was Sam. Sam was such a gentleman. He would always open the door for me when we arrived at church. The church gathered at night. The women sat on one side and the men on the other. I really enjoyed going to Spanish church. It was so nice to get to have this experience again. I missed Mexico so much, especially the culture and the way the people worship God.

Sam was an intern just like me, so we could hang out together, and it was okay. We continued to visit the Spanish church where one man began to take an interest in me. He asked for my number, and I gave it to him. To be honest, I really just wanted to practice speaking Spanish. His name was Pedro, and he was from Guatemala. He was a nice guy with a great personality. He tried asking me out over the phone in Spanish, and I told him that I was not interested in dating anyone at that time. This was because, I had begun to secretly have feelings for Sam, and I began to start feeling like he could be the one. Sam and I visited the Spanish church a few more times, and then we stopped going. I don't remember why we stopped attending, but we did.

I decided to test the five qualities on Sam, without him knowing, of course. He met all the qualities except for one. He was just so charming, and sometimes I felt like we were on the same page. We were even asked by someone if we were dating. He said, "No, she can do much better than me."

At that time, I didn't feel that way. I really thought he was something special, but God never let me tell him what I was feeling. I later came to find out that Sam had a pride issue. He also could be arrogant at times. This was a complete deal breaker for me. I was not interested in Sam after seeing that side of him. To be honest (and I know this sounds superficial), I also didn't care for the fact that his hair was thinning out. I like to play with guys' hair, and you can't do that if they go bald. My father has a great head of hair, and so does Jeffrey. I just figured because God knows what I like that He will give me what I like too.

Over the next couple of months, God began to show me that more work was needed to be done to prepare my heart for marriage. It did not help when I went home for winter break for a few days, and I saw Jeffrey. Jeffrey always had a way of melting my heart. I realized that I still had thoughts of being with him, but God had a way of fixing that.

Chapter 8

Fasting and Praying for My Future Husband

A month and a half had passed since I was last home and saw Jeffrey. I began to think about him and how much I missed him. Then God showed me that I needed to get rid of any thoughts of ever being with Jeffrey. He warned me that if I did not bury the thoughts of being with Jeff, then I would not get to meet the man I was to marry. He said that I needed to fast and pray for my future husband. This was to be done so that my heart and mind could be switched off of Jeffrey and switched on to accepting my future husband.

On February 18, 2007, I wrote this to God,

God,

I know that you are calling me to bury the idea of Jeffrey and I ever getting married. I am letting you know that I am accepting this. I will begin fasting for 7 days on February 26, 2007, through March 4, 2007. It will be a fast in preparation for the man I am to marry. I will focus on your love these 7 days. I will also focus on Scriptures that deal with marriage and ministry. I understand Lord that I am ready to make this commitment.

I trust in You, my God. Amen!

The next day on February 19, 2007, I wrote this to God,

Dear God,

I thank you for this grand opportunity to bury the thoughts of being with Jeffrey. I realize that Jeff and I will never be together. I have known him for over 9 years now and it's hard to imagine life without him. Lord, I could not live with him because it is not your will. I am therefore burying the thoughts and feelings of ever being with Jeffrey. I trust in your will for both mine and Jeffrey's lives. I pray that if he is supposed to marry Hannah that they would both treat each other with respect and kindness. Also that they would love each other with a godly love. I thank you in advance for what you are going to do in my life. I know that this week and next week will be a blessing to me as you prepare my heart for my husband to be. Thank you, Father, for your guidance in this matter and all other matters.

Your daughter,
Abigail Saba

Right before the fast, I decided to call Jeffrey on the phone. We talked for a while and laughed and laughed. I was going to miss him. He didn't know this, but I was not going to be calling him for a while as instructed by my Heavenly Father. Maybe I should have told him, but I did not want to upset him.

The first day of the fast was February 26, 2007. I did not do a complete fast in the sense of no water or food. I still had to work so I only ate crackers with a little bit of peanut butter and an apple for lunch. So I fasted two meals and ate a light lunch. That night, as I started to pray and fast. I began to give the Lord my thoughts and feelings for Jeffrey. I buried those thoughts and trusted God for what He promised me. Then I wrote this letter to my future husband.

> *To my future husband,*
>
> *I am praying and fasting for you this week. I know that God is beginning to show me different ways in how I am to commit my thinking. I used to think I was going to marry my best friend, Jeffrey Taylor. However, you are definitely the one I am going to spend the rest of my life with. I love you my dear sweet man of God. I love your admiration for God's will in your life. You are beautiful and I cannot wait to finally meet you. God is going to have so much fun working through us to do His will. Amen!*

Then on February 27, 2007, I wrote the following letter:

> *To my future husband,*
>
> *This is day two of the fast and I wanted this letter to be especially for you right now. I'm not sure what trials or temptations you are facing at this moment, but I know that God has a way of turning things around for the good. Hebrews 10:36 NLT says, "Patient endurance is what we need now so that we can continue to do God's will then we will receive all that God has promised to us." So keep strong and in good faith. You are going to make it. Trust in God for all wisdom and understanding. He will guide you through life's greatest adventures. I love you my dearest. Keep your heart pure as I wait for you, and*

I will continue to pray as God makes ready my heart for you. Amen!

And on February 28, 2007, I wrote:

To *my future husband,*

This is day three of the fast. Today God has shown me to surrender my anxiety to Him. I really want to meet you soon because I want to start my life with you. The vision that I have for ministering to others is something that I believe we both share. You are a true blessing that will be sent my way soon enough. Right now I am struggling with all the drama that the Mission puts a person through. Some students come straight out of high school, and it can be a bit overwhelming at times. I am here for a reason, and I must rely on God for understanding. He has a plan that I don't understand at this time. I know that God is working in both of our lives to will and to act according to His good purpose. I love your heart. Keep it pure for Christ. In Jesus's name, amen!

Today is March 1, 2007, and I am in the middle of my fast. So far, this has been a great experience as I feel so much closer to God and less connected to Jeffrey. I no longer have feelings or thoughts of marrying Jeffrey, and I feel like my heart is already falling in love with my future husband. I know that it sounds strange. How can I fall in love with someone who I haven't even met? I guess I am in love with who he is. I know that my future husband is a man who loves God, and he takes the Word seriously. I know that he is responsible, and we will have a wonderful life together serving God and others as a team. I could not have had any of that with Jeffrey. The idea of meeting my future husband was getting more and more exciting each day.

During the fast, God spoke to me and gave me two signs to show me who my husband will be. **The first sign was that I would recognize my husband by his heart before his looks**. I thought this was strange because as people, we usually notice others by their looks before getting to know their hearts. I even thought to myself, *What is he going to do? Carry some elderly person across the road?* I just could not figure that one out, but I was thankful for God's hand in all of this. **The second sign would be that we would become friends, then best friends very quickly, and our friendship would be founded on our relationship with Christ.**

After God showed me these signs, I was eager to meet my future husband. It was such a blessing to have God leading me and giving me these amazing signs to help me recognize my husband. This was such an exciting time in my life, and now I just needed to wait on God to fulfill all His promises.

Chapter 9

Prayer Letters To My Future
Husband Continued

*I*continued to write letters to my future husband daily
throughout the fast.

On March 1, 2007,

> *To my future husband,*
>
> *I feel like I am going to meet you soon. Life is
> going to be different for the both of us once we meet.
> I know there will be many challenges, but we must
> face them with boldness. I love you and I am praying
> for you. Come soon, let God be your guide to me.
> Remember to protect your heart. I hope that you
> are excelling in every area of your life. "Excellence
> honors God and inspires people" (Bill Hybels). May
> you be blessed with an abundance. I know that one
> day you will be a great blessing to me. In Jesus's
> name, amen!*

On March 2, 2007,

To my future husband,

Today you were really in my thoughts. I even thought about the process before marrying you.Obviously, we will take time to get to know each other and I am really excited to get to know you. We will also need to get to know each other's relatives. Be prepared, my dad is quite the warrior, but he will be nice. I know that you are a man of God. Your word is not from a babbler. You have a heart full of the joy of The Lord. I know that you praise The Lord with all your strength. I love that you have taken on the various tasks in your life. Bless your heart as things begin to change in your life.

I traced my right hand as a symbol of promise that my heart belongs to God first. You will have some of my heart. When we unite it will be a sweet promise fulfilled in which we will bear fruit. I love you and cannot wait for this day.

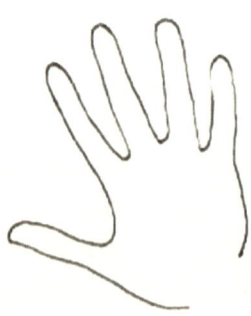

On March 3, 2007,

To my future husband,

Today I went through some trials. I feel ready to leave the Mission, but I can't. Instead I must stay in God and rely on Him alone. I am praying for you today that if you are going through any trials, you will be delivered in Jesus's name. Keep your head up and keep your eyes on Jesus. I can't wait to finally meet you! We will have a long life together serving God and the body of Messiah. Put on the shield of faith, the helmet of salvation, the belt of truth, the gospel shoes, and the breastplate of righteousness.

Dear Heavenly Father,

Please guide his heart to come to me. Let our lives shine among men, so that they may glorify You in heaven in Jesus's name, amen.

On March 4, 2007

To my future husband,

Oh, dear sweet man of God, this week has been such a blessing to my heart. I needed this week to get in tune so that I could be fully committed to marrying you one day. I cannot express how much thankfulness I have to God in words alone. I must use tears of gratitude, laughter, praise, and complete humility as I come before Him. I know that our lives are going to dramatically change once we meet. We are going to start a new adventure, a new chapter together as best friends and as partners in ministry. I love you. What more can I say? May your heart be filled with the joy of The Lord. I will see you soon! I leave you with this challenge. Stand up to your fears and make all things disappear. Let God be God so that He can do a work in your life and in mine. He gets the glory for our relationship. I am so thankful to my Heavenly Father for allowing me to one day join with you in marriage. Bless your dear, sweet, heart in Jesus's name, amen.

March 4, 2007, was the last day of my fast. I felt so prepared for what was to come. It was such a joy to think about what God was about to do in my life. I wrote two more letters to my future husband after the fast.

On March 6, 2007,

To my future husband,

God bless you in all that you do. May He keep you safe as you take these next steps in coming to meet me. I love that you have not given up. God is amazing! That is what He is. I hope that you see that today. Look around and just see how much He loves you. Trust in God for all things. I hope to meet you soon.

Your love, your friend, your partner for life. Jesus is life, Jesus is love, Jesus reigns forever so love Him forever and never give up on His beautiful name.

"Now it is God who makes both us and you stand firm in Christ. He anointed us, set His seal of ownership on us and put His Spirit into our hearts as a deposit guaranteeing what it to come." 2 Corinthians 1:21–22 (NIV)

On March 8, 2008,

To my future husband,

Today I pray that you stay focused on God's love. The love He gave you when He sent His Son to die on the cross for your sins. Open your eyes and see His love surrounding you. Do not fear, for the day belongs to God. Keep your tongue in check and be aware of what is going on around you. You are a brave soldier in God's army. Therefore stand strong and do not let anything move you. God's love provides strength, nobility, and guidance. If today you find yourself in a tough situation, run to Jesus. He will always help you. He has already promised that He will be with you till the end of the ages. Live your life with God in the driver's seat.

Love,
Your future wife in Jesus's name, amen.

This concludes my prayer letters to my future husband. Now it's time to get ready to meet him. I hope I will be completely ready now that my heart no longer is connected with Jeffrey's. I am so excited for the day that I get to meet my true love. It is going to be a miracle in the making. Thank you, God, for always leading me and guiding me on the right path. May Your blessings always be upon me and my future husband. In Jesus's name, amen.

Chapter 10

Meeting My True Love

*I*t had been a month and a half since I fasted and prayed for my future husband. I began to realize that I wanted to go back home and take classes for human services at the community college in my hometown. I did not want to spend another year as an intern at the Mission. I felt like God was moving me in another direction. However, I would have to return to Baltimore to take a test to receive my minister's license within the year. All I knew was that I wanted to get things moving in my life. I felt like I was standing still, unable to move. One special day changed all of that and helped me to get out of the rut I was in. It was the day I met my husband!

On one fine afternoon in the middle of April of 2007, I was at work. A man in his mid-twenties was looking for the quickest line in which to check out after picking up some items for his lunch. He chose my line as it happened to be the shortest at that time. While standing in line, he looked at me and had what seemed to be a vision. In the vision, we were at the park having lunch together like a family. He thought to himself, *That was strange.* He brushed it off and proceeded to my line to purchase his items. I was not paying a lot of attention to the young man. I talked a bit and then began to ring up his items. Then, noticing my name tag, he said, "I recognize your name. It's in the Bible."

All at once, something strange began to happen to me. My heart felt like it flipped inside of my chest. Now I know that this is not physically possible, but I do not know how else to explain it. I literally was in a temporary shock, wondering if there was something wrong with me. At the same time, I did not feel like anything was in pain, so I did not worry about it.

At that point, I began to wonder if this was a sign from God. Could this be the man I am supposed to marry one day? After ringing him up and he left, I could not remember what he looked like. That was the first sign. God told me, "**You will recognize your husband by his heart before his looks.**" I went back to the Mission that day and told my closest friends. Later that week, I also shared what happened to me at Celebrate Recovery. People asked me what he looked like and wanted to know his name. I said, "I don't know," to both questions.

My friend Jane said, "We'll just call him Target boy."

I laughed and said, "Okay."

I'm sure people thought I was crazy. I kept thinking about what his name was. I would go to sleep dreaming about the next time I would see him, knowing that God would reveal him to me if I saw him again.

Almost two weeks had passed when he entered the store again, and this time, my eyes were opened. I could see him, and I knew even before he came into my line that he was the one I was waiting for. When my future husband came to my line to purchase his items, I asked him, "So what is your name anyway?"

He chuckled and said, "I never gave you my name. It's Matthew." We talked for a bit more, but there was a lady in my line behind him. She was smiling at the two of us as we were talking. She probably recognized the chemistry between us. Anyway, I didn't want him to leave without getting my number. So I ripped off a piece of receipt tape and wrote my number down. I told Matthew, "I could always use another Christian friend. Here is my name and number." He smiled and took my number, and the next day he called me.

I was so excited to receive the phone call. It was utterly amazing! We talked for a while and laughed a bunch. Then we made plans to hang out in a few days at Subway after church. Now when people asked me, I could actually tell them what Matthew's name was and what he looked like. His name is Matthew Montgomery. He is tall with a great head of auburn hair and blue eyes.

Our first day hanging out was great. We ate a good meal and had a wonderful Bible study. We also joked around and made some funny things with the straws. Sometime during our time at Subway, Pedro from the Spanish church walked by and saw me from the window. He had a huge grin on his face and looked as though he wanted to come in and say hello. However, when he saw Matthew sitting with me at the booth, his head went down, and he walked away. It was sad to see Pedro so upset. I told Matthew that I met Pedro at a local Spanish church, and he asked me out to which I had said "No." Matthew thought it was interesting that he walked by at that moment, and I agreed. We continued to have fun getting to know each other. Time flew by. Before we knew it, we had been at Subway for five hours. I'm surprised they did not kick us out. We didn't want the fun to end, so we decided to meet up again later that night and go see a movie.

The Mission group was getting ready to go on a camping trip, and I was one of the interns who was staying back to help take care of the facility. When I left to go to the movies, it was late, 9:30 p.m. to be exact. We were going to see the last showing of *Spider-Man 3* at 10:00 p.m. During the movie, we joked around, and we decided that we should make up a goofy superhero. After the movie ended, we decided to hang out again in a couple of days. I told him I had a laptop if he wanted to try and write a funny story about a superhero. He really liked the idea, and so we began to meet at either coffee shops or yogurt shops to write our story. I also invited him to Celebrate Recovery and church on Sundays.

When Jane saw Matthew at Celebrate Recovery, she asked, "Is that Target boy?"

I just nodded my head and smiled. It was amazing to be able to share this experience with my friends about how God showed me the man I was to marry. Even though I just met Matthew, it was like I had known him for years. We became friends, then best friends in less than a month. This was the second sign that God gave me to recognize my husband. God had said to me, "**You will be friends then best friends very quickly, and it will all be founded on the relationship that you have with Christ**." This further confirmed to me that I would marry Matthew one day.

Chapter 11

Discovering Our Love
For One Another

I found out that Matthew had been praying for a really good friend who loves God. He told me that God answered his prayer by send ing me to him. I thought that was special for him to share that with me. I did not tell him what God had shown me concerning marrying him yet. I knew that I had to be careful with that information. I did, however, tell him about Jeffrey and how I had previously thought that I was supposed to marry him. I further explained that God was preparing my heart for marriage to a man who loves Him. Matthew told me that he was unsure if he would ever get married. I thought that sounded strange, and I left him many hints to suggest otherwise, but he never got any of them.

One day, I decided to finally call Jeffrey. It had been a couple of months since I had last spoken to him. I called him and explained that I was sorry for not calling him in such a long time. I was simply trying to process everything that God had spoken to me. I told him that I believe I had met the man I am going to marry. I also wanted Jeffrey to know that I still wanted to be his friend and that I would love it if he could meet Matthew someday.

Jeffrey said, "I feel like you have replaced me." At that point, I knew that things would never be the same between us. Our friendship began to dwindle, and our phone conversations stopped.

We would email sometimes, but that was it. I told Matthew about the conversation I had with Jeffrey (excluding the part about marriage, of course). Matthew thought it was interesting that Jeffrey said that I had replaced him. He did not say much about it. It could be frustrating at times to know that I am going to marry this man in front of me one day while he has no clue. I just kept praying to God to direct our paths and to open Matthew's eyes to see that we are meant for each other.

It had been a month since we started hanging out when I had to leave for a trip. I was going to Oklahoma with my parents to see my eldest sister, Laura, graduate from college. I told Matthew, "I'm going to miss you while I'm gone."

He exchanged the same sentiment and gave me a hug goodbye. I was sad to leave, but I had not seen my sister Laura in a long time. It was simply overdue. The trip out west to see my sister was great. My parents and I had a great time together. We stopped off at various stores, and we ate some great food, much better than what I had at the Mission.

While on the trip I told my parents, "I believe I met the man that I am going to marry."

My dad told me, "We'll see."

My mom was happy for me, and she seemed delighted at the prospect of meeting Matthew one day. I also told my parents that I was planning on being home and going to community college next year. They were excited about that.

When we made it to Oklahoma, my sister greeted us kindly and invited us to her friend's house for a gathering. Her friend, named Sara, was a devout Christian. Sara and I talked for a while. I felt led to tell her about what God had been doing in my life and how He had shown me who I was going to marry. She began to cry and tell me about her previous relationship and how it had been difficult for her to let go. Sara said that I encouraged her through my story to keep going and to leave the past behind her. She was going to start looking forward to what God had in store for her life.

My dad looked over at us talking, and seeing her cry, he said, "Abigail, why did you make her cry?"

Sara smiled and said, "It's okay. It's a good cry."

I felt blessed that I got to be a part of Sara's healing process. Yahweh had used my testimony to help her in her time of need.

We had a good couple of days with Laura, and then she graduated. It was a wonderful ceremony. We ate a nice lunch to celebrate the occasion, and then we spent the night and headed out in the morning back toward Virginia. When we got back home, I was so excited to get myself ready to head back to Maryland to see Matthew. I called Matthew and told him that I would be back in Maryland and that we should hang out when I get back in town. He was thrilled, and we met up as soon as possible. When I saw him, I gave him a big hug, and we went to the park and goofed off. We played basketball and chased each other in the park with dart guns. It was so much fun! We laughed and laughed; it was a wonderful day. I told Matthew about my plans to move back home at the end of June. He said, "Well, we better make the most of our time together as we only have six weeks left."

I told him I still wanted to visit him and that he could visit me as well. He agreed.

At the Mission, we were having our monthly meeting, and Pastor Robert asked all of us if we were planning on returning the following year. I told him that I would not be returning next year as I planned to go home. Pastor Robert was disappointed, but he understood. I also told them that I believed I had met the man that I was going to marry. I explained that it was not anyone from the Mission. The director laughed and said, "I know that none of these guys here can keep up with you."

I just smiled as I looked around at some of the male interns in the room. He was basically dissing these men. It was quite funny for me. Anyways, he was right about one thing: it takes a special man to be with me.

Over the next few weeks, Matthew and I grew closer and closer. It became so much harder to say goodbye. I never felt like this with Jeffrey. I could not imagine my life without Matthew in it. One day, Matthew stopped off at his house and introduced me to his dad, David. My first impression of David was that he is a gentleman with a great sense of humor. I could instantly tell where some of Matthew's character traits came from. It was nice to meet the man who raised my future husband. A couple of weeks later, I met Matthew's mom and sister. Matthew and I had stopped by his house before going out again to play basketball. His mother, Danielle, hails from Britain. She has a very dry sense of humor, and she can be very forthright at times. Matthew's sister Pamela came by for a visit with her two adorable little boys. Danielle is a very loving grandmother. She has really invested a lot of time into her grandchildren. Pamela is an extremely hardworking mother with a lot of ambition and drive to excel in just about anything she sets her mind to do.

Over time, people became skeptical of Matthew and me just being friends. At one point, Matthew overheard his parents discussing our relationship. He called and told me that his mom and dad believed we had to be more than just friends. Matthew said that they can believe what they want to believe; we know that we are friends. I added to the conversation and said, exactly. His parents were not the only ones who felt this way. In fact, one of the main leaders from the Mission suggested that I enter into a courtship with Matthew. I told him that we were not ready for that right now. We are just friends. I told Matthew about what I was told. He said, "That's funny. I guess people don't think you can be just friends with members of the opposite sex." I agreed.

During our last month together, we continued to do Bible studies, attend church and Celebrate Recovery, and write our silly superhero book together. At Celebrate Recovery, Matthew was asked to take over my position when I left, which was to help set up the projector and music for worship time. It was great to see how the Lord was using us both in the same ministry. We also went to the Medieval Times dinner theater. It was so enjoyable. We made T-shirts that said, "We are children of the King of Kings." We wore those shirts at the dinner theater. We also made other shirts related to the Bible. I cannot remember a time in my life when I had this much fun.

Getting to know Matthew and being his best friend was and still is such a blessing. He is such a humble man. He balances me out in every way. He also meets all the qualifications that I wanted in a husband. These further confirmed that he is the one for me. That being said, Matthew still had not realized that he was supposed to marry me. I had to leave soon to go back to Virginia, and I really wanted him to know that we were meant for each other. It had been so difficult to know that we were supposed to be together, and I could not tell him. I knew that God had to be the one to reveal this to him, and I could not wait for that to happen.

A few days before I graduated from the Mission, Matthew got into a car accident. Thankfully, it wasn't too serious. More of a fender bender at best. He had to wait for the insurance to give him a rental car, and he had some errands to do. Although Matthew never asked, I let him use my car. My car was packed full as I was getting ready to move back home. I picked Matthew up from his house and had him drive me to work. Then he came back to pick me up after work. He was so sweet; he filled my car up with gas, and he bought me a going-away present. It was a recorder. On our last day together before I graduated, we went to see a movie. During the movie, he put his arm around me. I was so excited about it, but I did not tell him. It was going to be so difficult to leave my best friend, but I knew that it was only temporary.

The next day at my graduation, Matthew showed up early. A friend of mine who had not met Matthew saw him reading the Bible. He said, "Oh, I see he likes to read the Bible like you do." I nodded my head yes. Both Matthew and I would sit down and read for thirty minutes to over an hour sometimes from the Bible. I interrupted Matthew to tell him that my parents were running late, and I wanted to see if he could make sure they knew where to go upon arriving. He agreed to do this for me. I really wanted to be the one to introduce him to my parents. Thankfully, my mother was friendly toward Matthew upon arriving, but my father just wanted to go in and have a seat. During the ceremony, Pastor Robert gave me much praise, not that I was asking for it. He told everyone that I had memorized most of the New Testament. Now it is true that I have a lot of Scripture memorized but not that much. I can usually tell you where a verse is when quoted, but not always. For that, I kind of just looked around like, "Okay," as people were staring at me.

After graduating and saying my goodbyes, I suggested that we get something to eat with Matthew. However, my dad had other plans. He wanted to go to a huge buffet that was an hour away. This was disheartening as I really wanted to spend more time with Matthew, and I wanted my parents to get to know him better. So after dropping Matthew off at his home, I got out and gave him a huge, long hug, and I listened to his heartbeat. I said, "I can hear your heartbeat. It is beating so strong."

He smiled.

I told him that I would miss him so much and couldn't wait to see him again. He reciprocated those feelings back to me. Then we said our goodbyes. My parents were looking on as my father wanted me to follow him to the buffet. My dad told my mom that I didn't need to get out to hug him when she knows we need to go. My mom told my dad she is going to miss him so just let them have their moment. My dad was not happy with it, and he yelled for me to hurry up. I stopped hugging Matthew and headed to my car to follow my parents. I was so sad. I didn't want to leave. I immediately began thinking about the next time I would get to see Matthew. After getting the okay from my parents, I invited Matthew to come to Virginia in a few weeks for a family reunion. He was excited and made plans to come.

When Matthew arrived at my house, I was so excited to see him. I gave him a giant hug. My mom made dinner, and Matthew was grateful to get to have Lebanese food for the first time. Our evening was nice together, and my dad was more polite this time. After dinner, we met up with my friends CJ and Jessica at the local pool hall. Matthew, CJ, and Jessica got along great. It was nice to see my old friends bond with my future husband. I used to hang out with Jeff, CJ, and Jessica. So this was definitely different but in a good way. Matthew and I had so much fun playing pool and joking around with them. After playing pool, we headed back to my parent's house and got some sleep.

The next morning, we got ready for the reunion. When we arrived at the reunion, I introduced him to my relatives, including my grandparents. The reunion was for my grandmother's side of the family, who is a child of thirteen. Honestly, I did not know all of my relatives there, but we had such a wonderful time, and I was glad that Matthew got to be a part of it with me. We ate some good homemade food, went swimming, and we even played basketball in the gym. We had a great time together. It was such a great day. I did not want it to end.

When we got back to my parent's house, we talked and relaxed from the long day that we had. The next morning, Matthew went to church with my mother and me; and after church, we went to get lunch. We once again regretfully had to say goodbye as he had to go to work the next morning. Thankfully, I would see him again in a couple of weeks. A couple of my friends from the Mission were getting married in Delaware at the beginning of August, and I invited Matthew to join me there, and he agreed to go.

Sometime after Matthew got home (toward the end of July), God had revealed to him that he was supposed to get married and that I was the one he was supposed to marry. Matthew called me and shared this info with me. I was so ecstatic. I told Matthew that I had known since May that I was supposed to marry him. I also revealed that I left him so many hints. He jokingly told me that guys do not take hints. I laughed and said how glad I was that he finally knew. We then expressed our love for one another and began looking forward to the day when we would begin our lives together.

Chapter 12

Blossoming Love

My friends' wedding day was in two days. I was excited for my friends, but I was even more excited to see Matthew. This would be the first time Matthew and I would see each other after confessing our love for one another. I carpooled with two other friends of mine from the Mission to go to the wedding. My friend Mary and I drove to Jenn's house and stayed the night there. The next morning, I called Matthew to let him know that we were on our way. The plan was for Matthew and me to figure out a place to meet on the way to my friends' wedding. We had figured out how to meet at almost the exact time. He kept checking in to find out where I was. Mary and Jenn told me that I was not spending enough time talking to them. I could not help it. I wanted to see Matthew so badly. Besides, it was fun laughing with him on the way to Delaware. Eventually, Matthew got pretty close to where we were on the road, so I asked Mary if we could stop at the nearest gas station. She agreed, not knowing my plan to meet Matthew there. Shortly after we arrived at the gas station, Matthew pulled up. I was so excited that I grabbed my stuff and rode with him. Mary and Jenn shook their heads and said, "You planned this."

I replied, "Yes, we did. We will see you later at the wedding." I know it seemed rude to do that, but when you're in love, you can't really help it.

When I got into the car, we held hands for the first time. It was different than holding hands with Jeffrey. Matthew is my one true love, so holding his hand meant so much more. Matthew and I went to the beach for a couple of hours before heading to the wedding later that evening. It was such a beautiful day! We had someone take our picture. We were wearing the shirts we made, which said, "We are children of the King of Kings." There was a place to change at the beach, and then we headed to the wedding. The wedding was outside, and the speaker system was not working properly so it was hard to hear my friends exchange their vows. Matthew and I began to talk about our wedding: things that we wanted and did not want. My friends' wedding was beautiful, and I was so happy for them. After the wedding, I was able to introduce Matthew to some of my friends from the Mission. Mary and Jenn began to joke around about my stunt earlier. Matthew and I just laughed.

After the wedding, I went to a movie with Matthew. Matthew put his arm around me while we held hands. It was comforting to know that God had given me such a kind and loving man who I would one day call my husband. I was going to have to say my goodbyes again and head home with my friends the following day. Thankfully, Matthew's employer had given everyone a fun day at Hershey Park with an extra ticket for each person. I was Matthew's extra, and I would see Matthew in less than a week. This time, I would be visiting him and staying at his parents' house for the weekend.

The day to leave for Hershey Park was finally here. I say *finally* because I could not wait to see Matthew. I felt so blessed to get to see Matthew again in such a short time frame. We were best friends in love, and we knew that we were going to get married one day. However, we did not know when or where we would be getting married. Not to mention we had only begun to express our love for one another in late July. This was still new to us, and we were not ready to share this information with others until we were in fact engaged. We wanted to go from being friends, to best friends, to being engaged, and then finally being married. Matthew let me sleep in his room while he slept on the couch in the living room. He is such a gentleman. We had only held hands at that point, and we would hug at times. The amazing thing is that we were both virgins. This meant that we would be united on our wedding day without any baggage from other relationships. It was truly a blessing from God that we were saved for one another.

The next day at Hershey Park, we had a blast. We rode all kinds of rides and spent time at the wave pool. Matthew introduced me to some of his coworkers, and we ate some Dippin' Dots ice cream. It was a joyous day! Later we went to get smoothies and wrote more of our silly superhero story. The next day, we went to church together, and it was great to see some of my friends who I did ministry with. Then we ate lunch together, and we talked about our future. Sadly, I had to return home, leaving my best friend yet again.

On the road home, I thanked God for Matthew. In less than a year, God had shown me who I was not supposed to marry (Jeffrey) and who I would be marrying (Matthew). It was so exciting to see how God was working in both of our lives to join us together one day in marriage. Our next visit would be on Labor Day weekend. This time, Matthew would be visiting me. Unfortunately, he would have to stay at a motel for a couple of nights since my parents would be out of town.

I started school at Virginia Western Community College shortly before Matthew's Labor Day weekend visit. I was so ready to study human services. I was also not far from receiving my minister's license from the Church of God. Helping people has always been part of my passion. I especially like helping women and girls who are in tough situations. I do not like it when women feel helpless in their situations.

I failed to mention this earlier, but while I was living in Baltimore, Maryland, I was blessed to be able to help start a ministry with a friend called "The Beauty Is in the Rose." This ministry was designed to help women to see the beauty within them. We had so many volunteers who helped with the ministry. Women who cut and styled hair, makeup artists, and one woman helped put together a really nice meal for the ladies. The ladies would come in and get pampered and then have a meal while a special guest would give her testimony. We would also hand out gifts to make the women feel special. It was such a blessing to be a part of this ministry. It was amazing to see how God was helping these women realize that they are valued, not for their looks but for who they are inside. The helpers also really enjoyed this type of ministry. It was basically a girls' night in which we also provided babysitting to mothers with children. When I went back home, I did not get plugged into ministry right away. I always found someone to minister to; however, at that time, I was more focused on my education.

The Friday before Labor Day, Matthew left home at 5:00 a.m. to come and visit me for the weekend. When he arrived, I was still at school and would not be able to meet him until lunchtime. Later, we went out to eat at a family restaurant called Famous Anthony's. Matthew and I sat beside each other in a booth so that we could hold hands and hug. We also took a picture together. Matthew brought his Wii with him so we could play video games later at my parents' house. He would leave for the motel every evening until my parents returned from their trip.

On Saturday, we went to eat lunch near a duck pond. After lunch, we fed the ducks. It was funny to watch the ducks fight over the food. We went for a walk in the park and held hands while talking about God and how amazing He is. We looked around and saw His creation from the mountains to the ducks in the pond and, of course, mankind.

Our Creator is wonderful and deserving of all praise. He gives us light from the sun, and He provides us with daily nourishment. He is always there for us, and God has promised us that He will never leave us nor forsake us. Matthew and I enjoy talking about God and His Word so much. After the park, I took Matthew to my dad's appliance shop. It was just down the street from the duck pond, so I figured, *why not*? After that, we went to the mall and walked around, and then we went to the Christian bookstore. While there, we ran into the pastor from the church that I attended with my mother. We talked with him for a bit about God and how everybody was doing. Then we went to go see a movie, and we held hands during the movie. I leaned my head on his shoulder. I felt so comfortable being with Matthew. Our love for each other continued to grow, and I could not wait to be his wife.

It was now September, and we were still discussing our wedding day. We didn't know when the day would be, but we were thinking after the school year. My parents would be returning home after their weekend getaway the next day. I really enjoyed our time together, just being us. Matthew and I played the Wii together that night at my parents' house, and then he headed to the motel for one last night. Matthew and I went to church the next morning. Then we went to a restaurant and went back to my parents' house and hung out until my parents got home from their trip.

My parents had a good time on their trip to the beach. My mom brought back some saltwater taffy for us to try. It was a nice treat. My dad wanted Matthew and me to clean some appliances at his shop on Labor Day for a few hours. My dad told Matthew, "You can see the shop that way."

I spoke up and said, "He's already seen the shop. I took him over there on Saturday after we went to the duck pond."

My dad was not pleased with me for taking Matthew over to the shop without his permission. I apologized. I did not think my father would be bothered by that. The next day, we helped my dad at his shop by cleaning refrigerators. Afterward, my dad treated us to lunch. It was nice to see how helpful Matthew was with the family business. In the evening, Matthew had to leave for home. One day, our home would be together, and we would never be apart again.

One fine day in September of 2007, I began to think about what day our wedding should be on. Without looking at the calendar, the date May 24th came to my mind. When I looked at the day, it was on a Saturday. When I got out of class, I told Matthew about May 24th, and he said, "That sounds good." We were both so delighted to have the date picked out. We both believe that God gave us the date of our wedding. Now that we had the date picked out, we needed to get the details of our engagement figured out.

One morning, before going to class, I ran into Hannah in the school parking lot. I was so surprised to see her as I did not know that she attended school there. Hannah and I talked about Jeff. She told me that she had lived with him for a while after high school. She went on to say that she no longer wanted to spend time around him as he had tried to interfere with her relationship with her current boyfriend. I told Hannah about the last conversation I had with Jeffrey and that he felt I was replacing him. She said that Jeff told her that I only called him when it was convenient for me. I told her that I cared about Jeff but that I had to move on. I went on to tell Hannah that I was getting married in May to Matthew. She congratulated me and said that we were both better off without Jeff as he can be toxic to be around. Our conversation ended on a good note. We were not best friends or anything, but it seemed like Hannah had found it in her heart to forgive me. I did not feel as though Jeff was toxic, but I understood why she said that. Jeffrey had been one of my closest friends longer than anyone else, and it was sad that he didn't want to speak with me anymore.

In the middle of October, I decided to make a trip up to Maryland to see Matthew and some of my friends from the Mission. During my visit, Matthew and I talked about when a good time would be for him to talk to my father about marrying me. After talking to my father, we could then get engaged and tell everyone else. While I visited Matthew, I kissed him for the first time. This was my first kiss. I never wanted to kiss a guy until I knew I was going to marry him. It was nice to know that I could be that comfortable to share that moment with him. I could not wait to share my love and my life with him beginning on May 24, 2008.

We decided that November 9, 2007, would be the day that Matthew would talk to my father about marrying me. This would be the start of it all. Matthew and I were so excited to finally get to this point. I did not know how my father would react. I am his baby girl, and he doesn't want anyone to take his baby girl away from him.

Chapter 13

Our Engagement

On November 8, 2007, my dad and I headed to Baltimore so I could take my test for the exhorter's minister license in the Church of God the following morning. I was nervous about the test because I was a full-time student, and adding this to my plate was a bit much for me. I felt that I could have spent more time studying if not for my other schooling. I was also nervous because of the conversation that Matthew would be having with my father as I took the test. I was so excited about the fact that the conversation was going to take place, but it came at a time when I needed to be more focused, and I was not.

When my dad and I arrived in Baltimore, we stopped off at the Mission. I went inside to say hello to some of my friends. My dad decided to wait in the car. Matthew showed up at the Mission and parked next to my dad, and they began talking. When I came out, I didn't expect to find Matthew talking with my dad, and so I laughed.

My dad said to Matthew, "Why is she laughing? Do you see anything funny?"

Matthew said, "I don't know why she's laughing."

I just smiled. I spoke with Matthew for a moment, and we set up a time to pick him up from his house the next morning on the way to take my test. Then we said goodnight and headed to the hotel. It was hard for me to sleep that night. I was not sure how I would do on the test and how my dad was going to respond to Matthew about us getting married.

In the morning, we went to pick up Matthew. He was going to ride back to Roanoke with us and stay for the weekend after I took the test. After I got dropped off to take the test, my dad went for a drive with Matthew. Matthew took my dad to a Mediterranean store, but as it happened, the store was closed. Matthew apologized, and they headed back. My dad then got a call from my sister Laura. He spoke with her for a little while. Meanwhile, Matthew was waiting to find an opportune moment to tell my dad about us. As they were about to get onto the Key Bridge, my dad finished his conversation with Laura. Matthew then thought to himself, *Now is the time to talk*.

Matthew told my father, "Andrew, I love your daughter, and I would like to marry her."

My dad paused for a moment. The silence was felt in the car. Then he said, "Well, I do not have any advice for you because it's not like my daughter Cara when she got married."

While it seemed as though my dad had not exactly given his blessing at that point, he also did not say anything against it either; therefore, it seemed like a positive sign.

When I finished my test, I was talked to by three pastors. I passed the Bible part of the test, but I failed the church history and church theology sections. It was such a bummer. I had to come back in January 2008 to take the other two sections. When I saw my dad, I told him and Matthew what had happened. My dad was disappointed, and I told him that I was sorry. I did not want to upset him as he had driven me all the way to Baltimore. The good news is that I would have more time to study the other two sections now. Next time, I would definitely pass the test. We then headed to Roanoke. My parents went to a movie that night while Matthew and I stayed at my parents' house. Matthew then "popped the question," "Well, do you want to marry me?"

I already knew that we were getting engaged that day, so this did not come as a surprise at all. I said, "Of course, I will marry you." He then put the ring on my finger. It was strange to wear at first as I am not much of a jewelry person.

When my parents got back from their outing, my dad saw me with the ring on my finger, and he said, "We're going to have a meeting."

My dad suggested that we wait for at least a year or two before getting married. We told him that we wanted to get married in May. My dad insisted that Matthew move to Roanoke. Matthew agreed. We had already discussed living in Roanoke as it seemed like a better place to raise a family. My mom jumped in and said, "Well, I am happy for you both." She gave us both a hug! My dad was more hesitant to completely accept our engagement, but he came around eventually.

The following week, Matthew visited again so we could attend my friends Zack and Chrissy's wedding in Lynchburg, Virginia. I was so excited for my friends as I thought they definitely belonged together. This would be the first time Matthew and I would be going to an event as an engaged couple. When we arrived at the wedding, we sat down beside some of my friends from the Mission. Matthew and I were holding hands, and my friends noticed that I was wearing my engagement ring. They were smiling and talking to one another about it. I just smiled and said, "Yes, we are engaged." They gave their congratulations, and then the wedding began.

The wedding was really sweet. You could tell that they were ready to begin their lives together. They were all smiles when the preacher said, "I now pronounce you man and wife. You may kiss the bride." Then Chrissy, who is much shorter than Zach, grabbed ahold of Zach and started kissing him. It was hilarious! The preacher who had young children there said, "Well, they are married now." Everyone laughed. It was a joyous day.

After the wedding, I got to see some friends who I had not seen in a really long time. I introduced Matthew to several of them. My friend Jenn saw us and said, "I knew it. I knew you two were going to get married." She gave me a big hug. Mary was there too, and she gave me a hug and congratulated us. Then I saw my friend from the Mission, Beth. I told her about our engagement while at the wedding and asked her to be my maid of honor. She gladly accepted. I was so thrilled to have her helping me on my big day.

After the wedding, we went to the reception and hung out with everyone. There were pictures everywhere of the wedding couple. It was definitely a beautiful day for my friends. Now we were even more excited and anxious to get to our big day.

After the wedding, as I had a whole week off from school because of Thanksgiving break, we decided to take the time to tell Matthew's family about our engagement, so we headed to Baltimore. After arriving, Matthew's father was the first to be told about our engagement. David was so happy for both of us. He gave us both a big hug, and he welcomed me to the family. It was a wonderful feeling to have such a warm and loving response from Mr. Montgomery. The next person to tell was Matthew's mother. When she got home, her daughter was with her. Danielle and Pamela were sitting in the living room when we told them about our engagement. Mrs. Montgomery's response was kind of funny. She said something to the effect of, "Do you expect me to be surprised! I knew you two were heading in this direction." His sister Pamela didn't say much to it. So like I said, it was strange in comparison to David's response. Danielle is British so maybe that is just the way it is. We also told several people at church about our engagement. We were invited to yet another wedding by some of our friends who attended Celebrate Recovery. Their wedding would be two months before ours.

For the next couple of days, I went with Matthew to work. I stayed in his car while he went inside and worked on printers. I had a lot of schoolwork to do, so when he went in to make repairs, I did my work in the car. It was fun getting to spend those days with him. On Wednesday evening, we left to go back to Roanoke to have Thanksgiving lunch with my family. It was wonderful to be congratulated by my grandparents, aunts, uncles, and cousins. We had a wonderful meal, and my Uncle Paul was making jokes as usual. He said, "I bet the reason that you didn't remember what he looked like is because he is too tall for you to see." He was referring to why I didn't know how to explain what Matthew looked like to friends after telling them, "I think I met the man I am going to marry." Everyone laughed. Matthew is six foot five inches, so he is used to people making comments about his height.

We had another meal to look forward to at my uncle Joseph's house that evening. My Uncle Joseph was about eight years older than my father. They were pretty close, and they loved to go hunting and fishing together. My Uncle Joseph and his wife, Patricia, used to always have gatherings around this time of year. They made some of the best Lebanese food, other than my mother, of course. Matthew really enjoyed the food, and we had a good time with everyone. They were all excited for us. My father was still a little cold toward Matthew. He just couldn't stand the thought of losing his baby girl. I assured him that I would always be his baby girl, but God brought Matthew and me together to be married.

A month had passed, and Matthew was getting prepared to move to Roanoke. He had to find an apartment, which was easier said than done. Honestly, he had a good job that he was leaving just to be with me. All we could think about was being together, and we didn't think about jobs. Matthew managed to find an apartment that was close to the college I attended. He had some money saved up, so he lived off of that until he found work. He worked a few temporary jobs, and sometimes he worked with my father at his appliance shop. I felt bad that he had a hard time finding a job that he wanted to do. He really wanted to work for a printer repair business like he did in Baltimore. He looked for this type of work, but it never worked out for him. Even though this burden was there, our love for each other continued to grow, and we could not wait for our wedding day to arrive.

We asked my grandpa to do the ceremony for our wedding, and he agreed. I couldn't be happier. I wanted my grandpa to do this. He has always been so special to me. My grandfather had been a minister in the Pentecostal Holiness Church for most of his life. He was also incredibly supportive of my decision to become a minister.

Over winter break, I had time to study for my minister's license. In January, Matthew and I went to Baltimore so that I could retake the parts of my exhorter's test, which I had previously failed. Thankfully, this time I passed. I was so thrilled as all I ever wanted to do was serve God. At this point, I felt like I would be blessed with more opportunities in service to Him. Matthew was supportive and happy for me. We got the rest of Matthew's belongings to move down to Roanoke while we were there. We took my Jeep, so we were able to get it all. His parents also gave us a coffee table to take with us.

The following month, we went back to Baltimore for Andy and Vicky's wedding. We knew them from Celebrate Recovery, and that's where they met. Andy and Vicky had a beautiful wedding. It was simple and sweet. We had many laughs with all our friends. We missed everyone so much. It was like a Celebrate Recovery family reunion.

When we got back to Roanoke, I decided to buy some cookware for Matthew, and we made spaghetti. Neither one of us was good at cooking, but spaghetti was easy enough to make. It would be many years until I mastered the art of cooking. Thankfully, we got to eat my mom's cooking every Sunday evening. It was a blessing to get to sit down together as a family. Matthew got to be a part of this special family time, where we enjoyed a delicious meal and had many laughs. My mother blessed Matthew and me by saying that she would take care of all the food and decorations for our wedding. We took care of the reservations and the church. My mom really wanted to make our day special, and so we agreed to let her do this for us. She is such a wonderful woman, full of such grace and poise.

My wedding shower was in April. All of my female relatives and friends who could make it were there. It was a beautiful day. The only boy there was my baby nephew who was born in October. He was so adorable, but he had been teething really badly, so his little shirt was wet. What a joy it must be to be a mother. I would have to wait a while longer to experience that joy for myself. It was different to be the center of attention. This was more special than any birthday party I ever had. It was a celebration of two people coming together to be made one. This was an early celebration; the real celebration wouldn't happen until the following month.

My mom had a cake made with a picture of me on it from when I was ten years old. She loves that picture, and after all, my mom was the one throwing the party. We played many games and laughed a bunch, though some of my relatives were extremely competitive. This was not a competition that I was used to. I am good at sports, especially playing basketball. This, however, was a game of "you can't say the word *wedding* or you get something taken away." It was fun to watch the women go crazy.

I loved getting to talk with my grandma at the shower as she was so encouraging. My grandparents had been married for over fifty years. They are the most wonderful people, and their love for each other is so beautiful. I soaked up everything that she had to say. With that many years of experience, you cannot go wrong. I received many gifts that day, and we hadn't even gotten to the wedding. After saying goodbye and thanking all of my friends and relatives, I loaded up the Jeep and headed to Matthew's apartment. He was surprised to see all the gifts we received. That was just the shower. I guess the saying is true that "when it rains, it pours." It was truly a blessing to receive all this love and support from our loved ones.

The wedding was just a month away now, and there was still so much to do. Thankfully, I already had my wedding dress. I had bought it a couple of months ago. We had already sent out the invitations, and we had some friends who were planning to sing at our wedding. We had been meeting with my grandpa for premarital counsel. My grandfather said that we were going to do well together. We loved being able to get advice from him. My grandpa was so gentle and caring as he gave us his blessing. If only my father could see what my grandpa sees. I guess he will have to accept that Matthew and I will be together forever soon. My dad wanted us to be happy; however, he did not want to lose his baby girl. I had told him many times that he was not losing me. He just does not like change. Nevertheless, this is the best kind of change, and I could not wait for my father to walk me down the aisle on my special day.

Chapter 14

Our Wedding Celebration

*M*y big day was almost here, and so much had happened within a year's time. I met Matthew through the leading of God's hand, and now we will be married in less than a week. My friend Beth would be here in two days as she was my maid of honor. We had some great times together in the Mission program. My bridesmaids were my sister Cara and one of my best friends from high school, Jessica. Matthew's dad, David, was his best man, and his two groomsmen were his brother, Josh, and his best friend from high school, Pete. I had a few friends who agreed to sing at our wedding. One was a friend I met while working at Target in Baltimore named Missy. In addition, my cousin along with a friend of ours from the Mission would be singing together. My niece Emily, who had just turned five years old was my flower girl, and Wesley, my soon-to-be nephew, who was also five was the ring bearer.

Everything was coming together so beautifully. All the bridesmaids would be dressed in a light-blue dress, and the groomsmen would be dressed in black suits with light-blue ties. My mother had prepared a lot of food for our wedding. She had made and frozen a lot of stuffed grape leaves and meat pies. She also planned and decorated a lot of the floral designs for the church. My mom poured a lot of time, energy, and money into helping plan our wedding. She wanted to make our day special. Matthew and I were (and will always be) so grateful for the hard work that she put into our wedding. Because of her efforts, our wedding day was nothing short of brilliant.

Matthew and I went shopping for gifts for our bridesmaids and groomsmen, singers, and, of course, my grandfather before our wedding party arrived. When Beth arrived at the airport, I went and picked her up. I was so excited to get to have her with me as she is such an important person in my life. When I saw Beth, I gave her a hug and thanked her for being there for me during this time. Beth was such a big help. She helped me with shopping and helped in the kitchen with cutting onions for the tabbouleh. She also painted my nails the night before my wedding. I am not the best at painting my nails, so believe me she was needed.

When Matthew's friend Pete arrived, he stayed with Matthew at his apartment. Pete and Beth helped at the church the day before the wedding. They seemed to get along well. Beth made a comment about Matthew and me as we were setting up the floral awning where the altar was. We hugged and she said, "That's enough you two. You need to wait until your wedding day." We both laughed. It was all in good humor.

Our other relatives would be here in a few hours for the rehearsal dinner. Missy called saying that she may not be there in time for the rehearsal dinner because of car trouble. I told her that was fine, and we'll work it out. The thought began to surface in my mind, *What if something goes wrong at my wedding? Will Missy be what goes wrong?*

Matthew and I bought subs for everyone for the rehearsal dinner. My friends Jessica and CJ had a surprise for us. They just got engaged. I was so happy for them. I got them to go to prom together, and now they are getting married. After dinner, we walked through the rehearsal. My mom's best friend Gabriella helped us organize the wedding. My niece was so cute with her little curls walking down the aisle. I could just picture everything the next day. My dad, however, was not smiling much due to a toothache. The strange thing was that Pete also had a bad toothache, and he, too, was not in the mood to smile. I, of course, was smiling from ear to ear. After the rehearsal, Matthew and I snuck out to the car to get the gifts for everyone. While outside, we kissed; however, we did not know that Matthew's older brother, Kevin, was outside in his car. He put the headlights on us when we kissed. We thought it was so funny. Kevin was funny like that. We headed back inside to give everyone their gifts. I had planned on giving Missy her gift also, but she was not there to receive it. After the rehearsal, we thanked everyone for coming to help celebrate our big day. This would be the last night where Matthew and I would not be together. We were about to say, "I do," and we would forever be united, just as God had ordained.

I called Missy again to see how she was doing. She said that she and her boyfriend would be in town sometime after midnight. I called Matthew and told him about what Missy said. He said that something was not right, and if she was having all this car trouble, she should not have come. I agreed. I really wanted Missy to sing at my wedding. She was a good friend to me while I worked at Target. She even came by on my last day at work to give me a balloon, a magnet, and a nice card. She was always singing gospel songs or other love songs. Missy's voice was so beautiful. It was about 10:30 p.m., and I knew I'd better get some sleep. My mom was wondering what was going on with Missy. I began to think it would have been better had I not invited her at this point. I went to sleep and around 3:00 a.m. Missy called and said she finally made it. I was shocked! She apologized for being so late saying that the car had all these problems. Anyways, I told her where the church was and that my wedding would start at 11:00 a.m. She said she would be there, but I had my doubts.

I went back to sleep for a few more hours. I woke up around 7:00 a.m. to get ready for my wedding. I had already packed my luggage for the honeymoon. We would be going to Orlando, Florida, and Clear Water Beach. Before the wedding, we had so much food to carry over to the church. My mom made grape leaves and meat pies. My dad and Beth made the tabbouleh. I had helped out wherever I could; however, I was not the best at cooking back then.

We arrived at the church around 9:30 a.m. I got my wedding dress on, and it was a little tight around my chest. Other than that, it fit. All of my bridesmaids got ready at the church. My sister Cara did my makeup and my hair. Jessica arrived around 10:00 a.m., and we all hung out while everyone began to show up between 10:30 and 11:00 a.m. The wedding photographer, Lisa, was also a friend of the family. She took over two hundred pictures. She began with us girls and then with Matthew and the groomsmen. My cousin Ashley and my friend Katherine had one song that they would be singing, but they said that they had prepared a second song just in case Missy did not show up. I called Missy around 10:45 a.m., and she said that she was on her way, but that she did not sleep long. She also wanted to know if she could get some money because she needed to fix the car. I told her that this was my wedding day and that I was not sure about what I could give her. She was not happy with that, and she hung up. I was asked again by my cousin and friend about playing the second song, and I said, "Yes, that would be great." I gave my cousin Ashley the gift card that was meant for Missy. She greatly appreciated it. Missy definitely disappointed me, but I was not going to let her ruin my special day.

It was now 10:45 a.m., and my wedding was about to begin in fifteen minutes. I had all these amazing feelings rush through my mind and body. I was going to be a wife and one day a mother. My friends and my sister encouraged me, and we laughed about some things. Laughing helped me to forget about the drama from Missy earlier. Several minutes later, my soon-to-be-husband went down to the altar. One by one, the ladies went down with the groomsmen. My dad was standing in front of my soon-to-be nephew who was the ring bearer, and Wesley seemed to be nervous. My dad encouraged him and said, "You are going to do great."

He smiled then walked down the aisle and stood beside Matthew. My niece Emily was so excited as this was her church, and she was not afraid at all to walk down the aisle. As she walked down the aisle, I heard people saying, "Aww!" Emily looked so adorable, tossing the flowers as she went.

Then it was my turn to walk down with my father. My dad wore a white suit with a blue shirt and a white tie. He looked so handsome. Unfortunately, he was not able to smile much due to a bad toothache. However, he made a good effort. I have walked with my father for over twenty years. He held my hand when crossing the street, protected me, and guided me just as a father should. Now he was about to hand me off to be married to Matthew. That was such an emotional time for both of us. I knew that Matthew would be a loving and supportive husband. When we got to the end of the aisle, my father kissed me and gave me to Matthew.

Now I was holding hands with Matthew as my grandfather began to speak. He started off by assuring the crowd that even though he had not officiated over a wedding in a long time, he was in fact licensed to perform marriage ceremonies. "I guarantee it," my grandfather exclaimed to the crowd's amusement before officially beginning the wedding ceremony. My grandfather proceeded to lead us through the ceremony. I had to remind my grandfather about the lighting of the candles. He said, "Oops, I forgot!" Everyone thought it was funny. My grandfather said some other funny things during the ceremony too. It was so wonderful to have him be the one to wed us. After we said our vows and exchanged the rings, it was now time for my grandpa to say, "I now pronounce you man and wife. You may now kiss your bride."

Matthew and I discussed kissing prior to our wedding day. We agreed that we would count for three seconds and then stop. We are not into PDA. We did just that. We kissed for three seconds and stopped. My grandpa said, "Congratulations, Mr. and Mrs. Montgomery!" Then a bunch of Lebanese women yelled, "Lalalalalalala!" Many of the Americans had never heard that noise before and were surprised. I had heard that at other celebrations including weddings and knew it was the way of congratulating us.

Now as husband and wife, we walked down the aisle, smiling at our family and friends. There seemed to be about 150 people there. It was beautiful to see so many people come out to support us on our wedding day. After we made it down the aisle, my niece put her arm around Wesley's arm and walked down the aisle with him. Everyone thought it was adorable. While we all waited for the reception to begin, we had our pictures taken. There were so many pictures taken of me and my husband and all of our relatives. It was a bit overwhelming, but the end result was having so many wonderful memories to scroll through whenever we want.

Finally, it was time to eat, and I was looking forward to all the good Lebanese food. Matthew and I were the first to get our food. As we sat down to eat, everyone else congratulated us while in line to get their food. At one point, my niece Emily came and sat on Matthew's lap and ate his tabbouleh. He was looking forward to eating his salad, but she is only five years old, and it was funny and unexpected. It also shows how patient he is with children. My friend CJ came and sat beside his now-fiancé Jessica. He was cracking up and making jokes the whole time. He was the unofficial member of the wedding party. Honestly, I would have made him part of my wedding party if I could. He is one of my dearest and closest friends. He was there for me before and after all my drama with Jeffrey. It would have been great if Jeffrey would have shown up today, but I guess it was too difficult for him to see me marry another man. I will never forget Jeffrey. There will always be some kind of love in my heart for him. However, that love does not and could never compare to the love that I have for Matthew.

After everyone ate, it was time to cut the cake. It was a beautiful white cake with blue flowers. My mom put this funny ornament on the top of the cake depicting a couple. The groom was trying to get away while the bride was grabbing him by the shoulders to prevent him from leaving. We fed each other cake and gave each other some punch. We kind of laughed as the thought of feeding each other seemed silly. After that, my father-in-law gave a beautiful speech; however, the mic was not loud enough, so only those around him could hear it. Others made a speech, and then it was time for me to throw the bouquet and for my husband to throw the wedding garter. I threw the bouquet, and a teenage girl caught it. It was weird as I thought only the adult single women were going to try to catch the bouquet.

Then it was Matthew's turn. I sat down in a chair while my father-in-law, David, put his hands over Matthew's eyes, and he took the wedding garter from my leg. Matthew had the biggest grin on his face when he tossed the garter behind him. I cannot remember who caught the garter as my eyes were fixated on Matthew and his huge grin. After that, we went outside while people congratulated us and blew bubbles at us. We did not want people to throw rice at us. Bubbles also have the advantage of being less messy too. While outside, my father spoke to Matthew. I found out that my dad had told Matthew, "If you ever hurt my daughter, I will bring you down to my height."

My Uncle John was there and said, "Why are you telling him that on his wedding day? He's a good guy."

Matthew laughed and said, "He loves his daughter, and so do I." While in the parking lot, Matthew and I had our pictures taken with different relatives. My uncle Paul gave Matthew the idea to put my veil on his head. Matthew and I took a picture together with him wearing the veil. It is such a funny memory that we can look at whenever we want. We spent more time talking to all our family and friends. After everyone left, we got changed. Then it was time for us to get all of our gifts, take them back to our apartment, and get on the road for our honeymoon. Many of our gifts were in the form of money, which was such a blessing to us. We hugged our parents and headed out.

Matthew rented a car for our honeymoon to Florida. When we finally got ready to go, it was about 2:30 p.m. We were so happy to begin our lives together. We held hands and kissed, and then we headed toward Florida. We made it as far as South Carolina before stopping for the night. Matthew and I had talked about our wedding night many times. The first thing we wanted to do was read the book Song of Songs. We wanted our wedding night to start off with God's Word. After all, God is the one who brought us together. We would not be married today if it were not for God working in our lives to bring us to this point. Matthew and I will always be grateful for the love that God has given us.

Epilogue

───────ᵕ∾◦∽ᵕ───────

As of November 2021, we have been married for thirteen years, and we have a wonderful son who is now eight years old. We have done ministry together, and we continue to study God's Word together. Currently, I am a stay-at-home mother. My son Ezekiel is homeschooled and is in the fourth grade. It has taken me a while to work on and finish this book. I felt like now was the time to get this done. There are so many marriages that are failing even among God's people. When a marriage fails, it affects more than just the couple. It often negatively impacts the lives of their children. Had I married Jeffrey, my life would not have been the happiest.

My advice and hope for everyone who reads this book is to seek God's will for your life. Start seeking Him now. He is there for you. He has promised you in His Word that He will never leave you nor forsake you. If you are young and reading this, I want to encourage you to pray and write prayer letters to God for your future spouse. Fast and pray with your parents' guidance and allow the Heavenly Father to show you what qualities to look for in a future spouse. God knows everything. He knows who you are supposed to be with. Let him guide you and reveal to you that special person. I pray that you will wait until your wedding day to become one with your spouse. It is such a beautiful thing to share together.

May God bless you as you seek His face and trust Him with one of the biggest decisions that you will ever make in your life, with the most important being to accept Jesus into your life to be your Savior. With repentance, we turn away from sin and turn toward God and His ways. As you live for God, you will be blessed. This does not mean that you will not have trials. Even through trials, we have a Savior; and as we call on Him, we receive deliverance. Trust in God for everything. May Yahweh bless you and keep you and make His face shine upon you in Jesus's name, amen.

About the Author

Rebekah Webb grew up in a Christian home and was taught to always help others in need. Through her parents' influence and direction, she began to seek after God at an early age. She accepted Jesus into her heart when she was seven years old and was baptized soon after. At the age of thirteen, Rebekah knew that the Lord was calling her to do ministry. At this time, she became bolder in telling others about Jesus. Upon graduating high school, Rebekah enrolled at a ministry school. During her tenure at ministry school, she was exposed to multiple forms of ministry and was able to tell many different people about Jesus. It was during this time that she discovered her passion for ministering to women. Seeing women with broken hearts from past hurts motivated Rebekah to help them. She mentored girls and women from all different walks of life and all different ages.

Today, Rebekah is a wife and a mother. She spends her time homeschooling her son and taking care of the home. She is very passionate about family values and is very excited to share her story of love and life with others. Rebekah is hopeful that her words will influence many people, all to the glory of God.

www.ingramcontent.com/pod-product-compliance
Lightning Source LLC
Chambersburg PA
CBHW021004150626
46549CB00012BA/1139